The Smart Girl's Guide to Self-Care

A savvy guide to help young women flourish, thrive and conquer.

Shahida Arabi

SCW Archer Publishing
scwarcherpublishing@gmail.com

Publisher's Note: This book is not meant for diagnosis or treatment. It is a
guide meant to supplement your self-care regimen. Please consult a mental
health professional for diagnosis and professional treatment.

Book Layout Modified from ©2013 BookDesignTemplates.com
Image Copyright © echo3005 // Shutterstock

The Smart Girl's Guide to Self-Care/Shahida Arabi. – 2nd ed.
ISBN: 978-1497489240

For my sister and my beautiful readers, for they too are warriors.

You must do the thing you think you cannot do.

−Eleanor Roosevelt

CONTENTS

1 YOUR BIGGEST BREAKDOWN IS

YOUR BIGGEST BREAKTHROUGH

Sometimes your biggest breakdown can be transformed into your biggest breakthrough. I've learned how to channel the pain from the past into success and stage my own victory. I want to help you do that too.

This book is meant to be a guide and a supplement for those who are deficient in their self-care regimen. It is meant to provide a useful introduction to learning more about mindfulness, radical acceptance, positive rebellion and strategies to cope with the trauma of emotional abuse. Many books, programs and psychological theories have influenced the writing of this book. As someone who has a background in psychology, sociology as well as a wide array of personal experiences with trying various mindfulness and therapeutic programs, this book is a distillation of the journey I've been through. A journey where I've tried to find the best ways to care for myself and love myself in moments of crisis and devastation. I wanted to write this book as a response to the many women I knew who struggled with similar trials and were determined to initiate positive changes in their lives.

Maybe you're dealing with more or less of the same. Are you in an abusive or unhappy relationship? Do you try too hard to please your friends at the expense of your own needs and wants? Are you subservient to the wishes of others and do you find yourself unable to become independent? Do you suffer from negative self-talk? These are all signs that your self-care regimen is lacking in some way.

My book attempts to answer these questions with practical practices and habits that will create a sustainable self-care routine. It will tackle some of the challenging questions that women in our society grapple with. How do you banish the browbeating bully inside your own head, influenced by all the bullies you've encountered in real life? How do you learn to be more present in the moment rather than ruminating over the pitfalls of your past? How do you learn to love yourself, despite all of the experiences that make you feel as if you aren't even worthy of your own respect and appreciation? The information in this book can help you with your healing, self-discovery and self-love in incredible, creative and effective ways. It can enable you to stage your own recovery, survival and victory in ways you never thought you could.

Young women are my target audience because it is even more difficult to convince young women that self-care is important. They are taught by falsehoods from the media and the norms of society that their needs and wants don't matter; that their relationships with others are much more important than the relationship they have with themselves. Yet all of our relationships with others are affected by our capacity for self-love, self-esteem and self-care. We cannot have healthy, happy relationships without first cultivating healthy, happy relationships with ourselves.

For those who are beginners to concepts like mindfulness, meditation, opposite action, reverse discourse, positive rebellion and radical self-acceptance, welcome! This is something we all have to make an effort to learn more about outside of school and work – regardless of whatever stage we are on the healing journey. These are skills you must obtain on your own by reading the literature, attending the seminars and doing your personal research. For experienced practitioners of these practices, I hope you'll find something new to mull over in this book. It's a patchwork quilt of all my experiences in learning how to cope with devastating losses, anxiety and depression. It integrates diverse techniques and practices to create a holistic program of tending to the self in healthier ways. Once we begin to channel our crisis into our transformation, there are no limits to what we can achieve.

I hope you will find some useful practices from this book to integrate into your daily self-care regimen. Each chapter ends with a list of supplemental online resources that will aid you in learning more about the strategies covered. You will also find a recommended book list at the end of chapter five. If you have purchased the print version of this book from Amazon, please note that you can receive the free Kindle version which will make accessing the links at the end of each chapter easier. You do not need a Kindle to read the book – simply download the Kindle app for free on your smartphone or tablet.

Remember – only you can take the first steps to engaging in better self-care. No one else can do it for you. The choice is yours and the time is now. I want you to know that the best remedy to any problem will always be found on the path of this self-love and self-care. In fact, it is often said that success is the best revenge, so let's start staging your own victory.

2 LONELINESS CAN BE A SPACE TO FLOURISH: CULTIVATING A SELF-CARE REGIMEN WHILE ALONE

I am going to state something blatantly obvious: self-care starts with the self. We might all have different definitions of what self-care entails: everything from allowing yourself a mid-afternoon nap to getting a massage at a luxurious spa. Maybe self-care for you consists of wrapping yourself in a warm blanket, a good book and a cup of tea every night. Or perhaps it looks more like going to a weekly yoga class or allowing yourself to cry, grieve and process all the emotions of a long, hard day.

Whatever image comes up for you when it comes to the definition of self-care, I hope we can agree on one thing. Tending to the self means not relying on the outside world to make you happy, but using its resources as instruments to aid and heal you. I start this book with a chapter on conquering loneliness and learning to be content with being alone because this is where my journey first began. I struggled with being alone. I didn't wish to be alone with my own hurtful thoughts. I was still reeling from all the hurt of the past and all of the traumas I had experienced from early childhood. Because I suffered from such a chronic sense of emptiness and loneliness as a result, I did many self-destructive things to fill that void as I emerged into adulthood. I entered and maintained relationships that I knew weren't healthy for me. I lacked a self-care regimen to take care of my emotional needs. These were painful traumas in my childhood that were repeating themselves in adulthood; as a result, I often gravitated towards toxic friends, partners and was extremely vulnerable to feeling lonely regardless of whether or not I was physically with people.

Then an amazing thing happened during my journey: crisis. A crisis I had never anticipated jolted me back to my life and I knew that if I was ever to survive and thrive, I was going to have to fight for my peace of my mind, no matter what the circumstances were. I had to channel my crucifixion into resurrection. I learned to cope with the stress and heartache of being alone in healthier and positive ways. I realized learning to be alone and loving yourself enough to enjoy your own company was one of the most fulfilling and fundamental things I could have ever done for myself. It gave me the space, time and opportunity to heal and revive myself in meaningful and productive ways. We are of course, social creatures - we do need the company of others to help support us.

However, we don't need people to validate our existence or love us in place of our own self-love. We don't need to be overly dependent upon others. This form of over reliance on others to 'complete' us actually separates us from our authentic selves and from others; it keeps toxic people in our lives long past the expiration date of unfulfilling relationships. It gives us the false belief that our happiness can only be found in others. It prevents us from achieving our goals by taking the focus off of ourselves and projecting our desires and expectations onto others. It enables us to avoid feelings from past traumas that we'd rather not feel. When we are starving for our own self-love and self-compassion, we are constantly looking to fulfill our internal needs with external realities. When these realities don't manifest, we feel unhappy, unfulfilled, and unwanted. We lack the self- knowledge allows us to see exactly how being independent and self-sufficient is vital to our well-being.

Maybe you're also afraid of being alone. Maybe you're in a toxic relationship not because you want to be, but because you're afraid of what will happen if you choose to end it. This could be a friendship, a romantic relationship or an unsustainable work partnership. Chances are, you might have more than one unfulfilling partnership in many of these areas. No matter what type of relationship it is, it is one where ties need to be severed and communication needs to end or be kept at minimum. It is hurting you more than it is helping you. It's causing you unnecessary stress and making it more difficult for you to fulfill your goals and destiny.

That is not to say that feeling alone is not a valid or useful emotion. Every emotion is a signal that motivates us towards change and loneliness is no different. Loneliness is not the same thing as being physically alone. This is an important distinction. Many people feel lonely even in a crowd, sometimes even lonelier when they are with people - especially if those people do not meet their needs. We can cope with loneliness in self-destructive and negative ways, or we can choose to rechannel this emotion into productive, positive outlets that help advance our goals and improve our overall mental well-being.

Loneliness is a signal which can tell us when:

Our emotional and psychological needs, for whatever reason, are not being met at the time. Usually this is due to a lack of psychosocial resources like a strong support network. These needs include the desire to be loved, respected, listened to, and wanted by others.

We are lacking in a sense of community or close bonds with the people currently in our lives. These bonds may have been disrupted by conflicts or otherwise underdeveloped. Individuals who lack self-confidence or self-esteem are more likely to engage in maladaptive interpersonal habits that ultimately sabotage their relationships and prevent new, healthier ones from forming.

We do not enjoy our own company. This can be due to low self-esteem, poor quality of self-care, repression, avoidance or unhealthy expression of significant turmoil and emotional hurdles. We do not like being by ourselves because we are afraid or pained by our own internal landscape, that of the mind.

A significant life event, such as the end of a relationship, can also evoke a sense of overwhelming loneliness and depression. Important biochemical processes helped create an attachment to this person and now the source of the attachment is gone. Many people underestimate the biological underpinnings of the effects of loss. Relationships often serve as a source of social zeitgebers, external cues from the environment that regulate our internal biological cues (Ehlers, Frank and Kupfer, 1998). When we lose someone we used to lie in bed next to, speak to first thing in the morning, our circadian rhythms are deregulated and this makes our bodies vulnerable to depression.

This depressed state is maintained by negative, cognitive distortions. Rumination over loss and engaging in negative thoughts about the self, the future and the world can perpetuate this emotion. Our negative mood becomes sustained by an endless cycle of increased attention to negative stimuli, memory biases that selectively remember the negative points of the relationship, and cognitive distortions which connect the ending of this relationship to indications of our self-worth and ability to form healthy relationships (Gotlib and Joorman, 2010).

A trauma of any kind can interfere with our executive functioning, disrupting memory, learning and decision-making. It can cause us to become socially anxious and isolated, as we begin to alienate ourselves from the world as a coping mechanism. Without reaching out to our support networks, our sense of helplessness and hopelessness can become intensified. We can feel unbalanced as our brains struggle to make a coherent narrative of our thoughts, memories and emotions, which can become fragmented and repressed after a significant trauma. Professional support is needed to tend to the effects of trauma, as well as the side effects it has on interpersonal effectiveness and relationships.

To cope with loneliness, steps can be taken to ease the overwhelming pain of this emotion and rebuild a better foundation for channeling this emotion into constructive outlets. These include the following:

1. Discovering a productive, positive mode of expression.

Creative writing or art helps us to reflect on our emotions while simultaneously converting them into works of art, works that we can be proud of. Studies have shown that art therapy used in conjunction with regular therapy can help trauma victims suffering from PTSD (Morrissey, 2013). There is an element of great satisfaction in the process of production and transformation, since we can witness how our emotions can create something innovative and useful, perhaps something that can be shared with others as well.

This also gives us a sense of empowerment and control; we control the art, so we decide the interpretation of events on paper and give fresh meaning to significant life events. It can also help to distract us from these life events by crafting a fantasy world we can escape into, temporarily, to give us space and distance from conflicts so we can return to them with a broader perspective.

Blogging and writing gives us an audience to share resources and ideas, which means we can share our work with others while simultaneously working on our own development. Not only can we help others coping with the same struggles by lending a helping hand, we also receive feedback on our own experiences. It creates a virtual community in which our work can potentially thrive and affect the ways in which others perceive their own lives and themselves. Some great blogs I follow are Baggage Reclaim (all about self-esteem, dating, relationships) by Natalie Lue, Getting Past Your Breakup by Susan Elliot (the ultimate guide to grieving and loss), and Good Vibe Blog (themes include gratitude and positive thinking). You can find the links to all of these at the end of this chapter.

Volunteering brings us into direct contact with populations in need and reminds us that there is a larger community out there that needs to be served. Volunteering reminds us we are not truly alone on this journey and that there are people who are less fortunate than we are who require our help. Volunteering gives us a sense of gratitude for the basic needs that are being met in our own lives. Volunteering often helps to give us a sense of larger purpose as human beings and enhances our overall awareness of the universality of human suffering. Visit websites like idealist.org or NYCares (if you're in the New York area) to search for opportunities available to you in your community.

Working on academic and professional success. We can use our loneliness to fuel our long-term goals. Taking small steps to meet our long-term goals makes us happier and more motivated, which makes us great company to ourselves. Start by using a two-page goal outline, a list of things you want to have accomplished by the end of this year. Underneath each goal, write down smaller steps you have to do this week to get a head start.

Once we begin that dialogue with ourselves of the goals we want to pursue, we increase our motivation to engage in better self-care and refocus on our own advancement.

Learning to do something new or improving at an already existing skill (e.g. knitting, skiing, filmmaking, etc). This adds to our emotional toolbox and makes us feel self- efficient. Once we gain new hobbies, we feel more comfortable venturing outside of our comfort zone and even prefer the solitude that enables us to engage in our new activities. It can also help push us to join communities centered around these activities.

2. Finding New Communities, Strengthening Existing Ones and Walking Away from Unproductive Ones

Evaluate which communities are worth investing in and which will provide a positive return on the investment. This means critically and honestly looking at your existing communities (this could be a group of friends, a church you belong to, or a support group or organization you're a part of) and understanding the ways in which these communities have met or failed to meet your needs. What is it about this community that is lacking? Is there something you can do to enhance your contribution to this community (e.g. speaking up more, making your voice heard?) or is the community ultimately unable to validate your needs/experiences? If the latter, you should not feel obligated to invest too much of your emotional and psychological energy into these communities.

There is nothing wrong with spending less time with people who make you feel worse about yourself or feel disconnected with because of some sort of incompatibility

– sometimes such interactions are unavoidable and even necessary like in the workplace, but many times we do have the power and control to choose who we spend our time with. Your time is valuable and precious. With the exception of family or work, which can be a more complex and nuanced issue to navigate, there is no need to harbor feelings of guilt or obligation because you do not wish to invest in a particular existing community that does not serve you. It may have served your needs in the past, but it may no longer be sustainable for your future.

Find innovative ways to meet people. Go outside your comfort zone to meet people you might not meet in your usual settings. Write down a list of places you often frequent and for one week, tell yourself to avoid them and find alternative places so you encounter new people. You might not meet your best friend at the new coffee shop you visit, but even just the appearance of a new barista might brighten your day in unexpected ways. New people means new experiences and can potentially enhance your social skills, challenging you to interact with various types of personalities and navigate unfamiliar settings with newfound confidence.

These small steps can lead to bigger ones for when you really want to engage in concrete actions to find new communities. For example, Meetup.com is a popular website that brings people together based on common interests, activities, and goals. After you've taken your baby steps of interacting with the unfamiliar in local settings, Meetup can be the practical next step to putting your skills to practice, meeting new people, getting in touch with new or old passions, and stepping outside of your comfort zone. If possible, limit or remove interactions with toxic people that are already in your life as well as any new ones you might encounter.

Now, what do I mean by "toxic people"? Sometimes, it is easy to recognize which people would be considered "toxic" to you and your mental health. Toxic people can be people who conspicuously leave a negative impact with their emotional, psychological, verbal or physical abuse. However, some toxic people are not as easily recognizable. They can be more covert and insidious - emotional vampires that are usually self-absorbed or unwilling to take the extra mile to give you the love, compassion or care that you truly deserve. Some may even outright disrespect or worse, abuse you.

Toxic people can be dangerous to your mental health because they emotionally exhaust you to the point where you limit your own self-care. When we are involved with toxic people, we find ourselves in non-reciprocal relationships where we are giving/investing way too much but receiving little to nothing in return. Get these people out of your system and kick the bad habit of keeping bad friends around just because you feel lonely. Just like the previously mentioned failed communities, they do not have any positive return. It would be better to spend time alone reflecting and working to improve yourself rather than to spend time with people who make you feel worse about your life. While it can be difficult to spot toxic people at first, here are some telltale signs you can remember to become more discerning in your friendships and relationships.

The Smart Girl's Guide to Recognizing Toxic Friends: Top 10 Signs

1. They are not happy for your accomplishments. When you mention your success, your friend's face goes automatically sour. She may look like she's eaten an entire lemon as she struggles to say congratulations. Or you receive a totally blank facial expression and no response at all, just a stare. She may even attempt to "one-up" you by mentioning her accomplishments quickly before you've even finished your sentence. This is the type of friend who is never happy for anything you do, and is secretly hoping you'll fail so that she doesn't have to feel so badly about her own life. This is toxic because real friends celebrate each other's accomplishments, and even if there is any jealousy involved, they will put it aside in order to congratulate their friends. Instead of feeling despair or pathological envy at their friends' accomplishments, true friends will be secure in their own accomplishments, and thus feel celebratory, inspired and motivated to better themselves when they hear about the accomplishments of others.

2. They covertly put you down. If you're happy and cheerful for whatever reason, toxic friends find ways to rain on your parade by introducing little storms and tempests of invalidation, belittlement, and degradation. These are often disguised as "helpful" or "honest" comments that actually have no value at all except to make you feel less proud of yourself. Saying things like, "Oh, anyone could've done that," when you mention something you accomplished or, "That's not a real major" when you mention your academic concentration. They also seem sadistically happy when you're failing or when you're going through a difficult time. This is a sign that something is seriously wrong with them. Real friends don't attempt to criticize or put down people just for the pleasure of making someone seem small. Only morally inferior and character disordered people do that in order to elevate themselves. If you can't be your greatest, authentic self around your friends without being constantly demeaned by them, then they're not your true friends. They're malignant bullies and narcissists. Get it straight and know the difference.

3. They emotionally exhaust you. Have you ever had this experience? You're on the phone with a friend. You ask your friend how she's doing, and find yourself being "talked at" rather than "talked to" for hours on end – and this consistently seems to happen all the time. As you finally get your chance to speak, your friend suddenly needs to get off the phone because she is now so tired from all the "talking."

Sure, we all have to vent sometimes and talk about ourselves. Certain situations warrant this type of behavior such as a break-up, a loss in the family, or any other traumatic event. However, if this happens quite often and you rarely get a chance to have a reciprocal conversation with a person, you're acting as their audience to a monologue and not as a friend. You also deserve to be listened to and deserve to talk about any problems in your life. Don't let these toxic friends convince you otherwise. Stand up for yourself and tell them this is an issue. If they continue to do this despite you establishing that boundary, it's time to forfeit the friendship altogether.

These toxic friends drain you and your ability to engage in self-care because they are emotional vampires whose only focus is them, their lives, their wants and needs. You don't exist, or if you do, you only exist in relation to them. For example, if a friend hears your traumatic story and uses it to turn the conversation back to her life constantly, this is a red flag for narcissism, so be careful. Real friends would listen to your story and make sure to give you feedback that is helpful to you before turning the conversation back to them. Stay away from any people with whom you don't feel there is an equal, reciprocal exchange of conversation, validation, compassion, and respect.

4. They are there for your good times, and never for the bad. We mentioned in #1 that you should stay away from people who don't celebrate your accomplishments. One caveat though: watch out for toxic friends who are only there to piggyback on your success. These friends only appear when you're doing very well, and rarely show up when you need them during hardships. They use your presence to associate themselves with you, for the sole purpose of seeming more important via affiliation to your success. Or they enjoy your presence only when you're in a good mood and they need you. Otherwise, when you have a health scare, or someone in your family has an accident, they are nowhere to be found. Real friends help each other through tough times and are there for each other even when times are challenging.

5. Not emotionally responsive, validating or helpful. What is the point of having friends if they can't even respond to your emotions? If you find yourself dealing with a friend whom you can have great intellectual conversations with, but only hear the sounds of crickets when you tell them you've had a bad day or you just had a breakup, this friendship is a no-go. Feel free to keep those type of people for your LinkedIn, but not for your real life crises. At most, they are a professional or academic connection because all they can do is talk about things related to the mind but not the heart. Sure, some situations lead to a loss for words, but real friends should be capable of basic emotional support, even if it's a hug and the words, "I am here for you." If your friend happens to be very emotionally invalidating, constantly telling you to "get over it" when you're going through a difficult time or gets angry at you expressing your emotions, leave them forever and don't give them access to your life in any way. They don't deserve to be your friend. Real friends validate each other's emotions while still empowering each other's personal growth.

6. They don't stand up for you. When an outsider or mutual friend makes a snide or insulting comment about you or does something hostile or horrific to you right in front of these toxic friends, you rarely see these toxic friends jumping to the rescue. They don't advocate on your behalf even if they are the only ones who can. They don't support you when you most need it. Real friends come to each others' aid; they don't have to "pick sides" in order to point out wrongdoing and consider your feelings. And also, when did we become so resistant to "picking sides"? Why shouldn't friends advocate for victims or call out inappropriate behavior when they see it? These toxic friends will more likely either stay silent or even participate in the belittling behavior on your behalf. That's when you know it's time to stop making excuses and stop defending people who won't defend you.

7. Their ego is bigger than their bond to you and they attempt to put a shade on your light. These types of friends are extremely narcissistic, jealous and they will do whatever it takes to maintain their delusion of grandeur. For example, they might refuse to compliment you when you're all dressed up, but compliment someone next to you who is wearing sweats and a t-shirt. They might put up pictures of themselves on social media with other friends, but avoid putting up pictures of you and them together because they think you outshine them in some way. Or they may hide or belittle your accomplishments to others while they brag about their own. These are superficial friends who can't stand having someone outsmart them or be prettier than them. Real friends appreciate each other's unique beauty, intelligence and charisma. They don't attempt to obscure your light in the darkness just because of their own place in the shade.

8. They only communicate through the screen. For this, I am referring only to "offline" friends who you have met face-to-face with. I know there are many online friendships that are built through supportive forums and I don't mean to diminish the value of those. However, for friendships that developed face-to-face and for friends who live within a reasonable distance of each other, there's no reason that both people in the friendship wouldn't make an effort to see each other in real life occasionally. You know, step away from the messenger and Facebook once in a while to actually make a face-to-face connection when possible. Be very wary of any friends who don't have time to see you, but seem to have all the time in the world to be wrapped up in their new boyfriend or girl posse 24/7.

These are not your real friends. These are buddies constantly talking to you through a screen, and electronic communication is often a cop-out for emotionally unavailable people. If these friends emotionally exhaust you as well, they have no place in your real life or even on your messenger list. You might as well be engaging with the wall, although the wall will probably be more sympathetic and won't hurt your feelings. Think of it this way: you're wasting energy on these toxic people by constantly engaging with them online because they won't grace you with their presence offline. They have shown you they don't have time to do a simple meet and greet by taking a step outside, so why should you hurt your eyes or strain your fingers for them? Real friends make the effort to meet in person; emotional vampires, like real vampires, can't stand the daylight and prefer the light of the computer screen.

9. Too busy for everything and anything. Related to #8, if your friend is constantly always too busy to see you or make any type of contact, especially in the midst of a crisis, *run*, don't walk away from the friendship. Yes, people have jobs, lives, and relationships to deal with. Nobody can always be there for you every time you need it. That's all fine and dandy, but if a friend rarely even follows up on how you're doing when you really need them and plays this "too busy" game consistently, this friend needs to get the door slammed in his or her face the next time he or she comes around looking for any attention.

Also, thankfully for technological advancement, social media has made it quite easy to assess whether these friends are truly "busy" or truly bullshitting. If you see your friend claiming to be too busy to call you during a crisis but posting statuses or liking people's posts on social media all the time, you have further confirmation that this friend is not a real one. Thanks, Facebook and Twitter for the heads-up!

10. Betrayal, breaking boundaries and disrespect. I saved this for last but it's the most important. If your friend disrespects you by: being flaky, multiple cancellations, chasing after or flirting with your significant other, calling you names, cursing at you, bullying you, coercing you, making you cry during an already rough time by being insensitive, pressuring you to do something, gossiping about you, or treating you with anything less than respect or consideration – it's time to take your fabulous self out the door. There will be plenty of people in the world who won't make you feel that way, so why not save your energy and invest in something that will have a positive return? You may as well spend that time investing in yourself and your big dreams instead.

Life is way too short to waste our energy on toxic people, whether they be friends or romantic partners. Learn to recognize these signs and you will pave a better path to a healthier life, better support system, and more meaningful as well as authentic relationships. Once you've experienced an authentic friendship with love, care, compassion and respect, I guarantee you'll never want to go back to one with the absence of these qualities.

Engaging in Concrete Self-Care Activities

It is important to engage in activities that remind us that we are worthy of care and investment. We must care for ourselves before we can take care of others. Here are some ways you can invest in the one thing that will consistently have a positive return: you.

Daily Meditation helps to improve psychological, emotional and even physical well-being. It pulls you back to the present and enables you to focus your attention completely on your own body, emotions and thoughts. There is a misconception that meditation is only about emptying the mind, but rather, it is about replenishing it and refocusing it. Studies show that meditation literally changes crucial neural connections in the brain that enable us to cope with sensations of anxiety, allowing us to respond to stress more productively so that we are more prepared to cope with challenging situations (Brown and Ryan, 2003; Creswell, Eisenberger, and Lieberman, 2007; Gladding, 2013).

Meditation will be one of the most powerful tools in your self-care toolbox because it is something that you can do for the rest of your life, on your own, at any time, for any duration of time and for no cost. There are also so many different types of meditation that you are sure to find one that suits you and your needs. Everything from guided visualization to body scan meditations – something fitting for each situation.

Many contemporary podcasts incorporate mindfulness exercises which bring us back to present moment and increase our awareness, remaining open to experiences without judgment. Mindfulness is the act of bringing our attention back to the present and is essential to the process of meditation. Meditation podcasts are available for free on iTunes and also everywhere on the web including YouTube.

I personally love the **Meditation Oasis** podcast by Mary and Richard Maddox. Mary's voice is so soothing and her podcast has many different themes to help you cope with various emotions and circumstances. **The Society of Australia** also has a very spiritually centered podcast called **Learning to Mediate**. These meditations are much more philosophical and lead you to envision different situations to bring you to a higher state of mental and spiritual clarity. **Michael Sealey's YouTube channel** is also a popular go-to for those who want to go into deeper, meditative trances to target and reprogram harmful subconscious beliefs.

You do not need to pay a cent to meditate on your own, although you can also seek out meditation centers that have a suggested donation fee if you wish to work with a professional or a broader community. I am very lucky and grateful to live in New York where there are multiple centers available – all of them are friendly, welcoming and perfect for meditators at all stages of their self-care journey.

If you live outside of a big city, however, you might have to do more digging. Start with a simple google search for meditation or yoga centers in your area. If nothing comes up, try spiritual centers and see if they offer any courses on meditation. After you've tried some podcasts, watched some videos and attended a How to Mediate class or two, you should be comfortable utilizing this practice on your own more often and creating a daily routine that's effective for you.

Yoga not only improves physical well-being but also lends to a sense of inner calm similar to meditation. It strengthens your body, improves your flexibility and relieves stress. If you are struggling with health issues, yoga can be an amazing way to re-energize your body and help enhance its endurance. You can seek out places to learn yoga by Googling or Yelping centers in your local area and also practicing at home with free videos and podcasts. There are so many types of yoga out there - candlelit flow yoga, aerial yoga, power yoga, Budokonyoga, Bikram, hot yoga or regular Vinyasa yoga - that I have no doubt you will want to explore all of them and find the right one for you. I myself enjoy Hatha yoga which sustains intense poses and focuses on integrating meditative breathing to relax tension in the muscles. It leaves me feeling lighter, self-confident and relaxed. I feel like I can conquer anything.

I hope this will be the experience for you when you try yoga (please start with beginner's yoga if you're new to it, to avoid injuries or complications). If you have injuries, you may want to consider some form of restorative yoga instead, where the focus is more on restoring the body rather than pushing it beyond its limits. Yin yoga and yoga nidra – two forms of yoga that focus on prolonged stretches, with yoga nidra taking you into a deeper meditative trance via visualization – can be very soothing for anyone who is struggling with ruminating thoughts or stress.

Or, if you're already an experienced yogi, take this time to push yourself to the next level. Go on a yoga retreat offered by the centers in your local area, or try a new form of yoga you haven't explored yet. Depending on where you live, there might be free or low-cost yoga classes (such as the popular Yoga for the People center in NYC) available. Groupon, LivingSocial and Yelp deals will usually have great discounts on yoga and fitness courses. Don't let the cost of yoga or any fitness class scare you away – where there's a will, there's a (low-cost) way to pay.

Exercise is an obvious one but it's something most individuals take for granted. As you know, exercise releases endorphins which boost mood and encourage a healthier lifestyle. Establishing a weekly or daily routine of exercise can seem daunting: not everyone likes running on the treadmill. Fortunately, there are so many ways of exercising that there are also infinite possibilities of how to make it fun. Make the time daily to walk, run, dance, or cycle.

For example, I've taken Broadway Dance Cardio classes that based choreography on the music from Broadway shows. I've also taken high-intensity dance cardio classes with a live DJ, did a pole dancing class and even a few Hip Hop and Burlesque dance courses (needless to say, these were my favorite). Picking these creative classes was a unique way of getting me energized and made me look forward to the class because it was so creative. The opportunities for creatively exercising are endless especially if you live in a metropolitan area, so don't underestimate these possibilities. Do what suits you and your particular needs, but make it a part of a daily or weekly practice so you do not lose out on its powerful natural effects. If you feel stagnant and unable to get off the couch, motivate yourself by turning on your favorite music and dancing during commercial breaks while watching television. Hey, we all have to start somewhere, and every energetic movement counts!

Good nutrition is not just about improving physical appearance. Knowing that we are eating healthfully and mindfully gives us a better sense of control over our lives, increases our sense of self- efficacy and becomes a significant part of our self-care. When we take care of our bodies, we communicate to ourselves that we are worthy of respect, care, and compassion. Many illnesses and diseases rely on the mind-body connection and healing is a holistic process that involves consistently healthy eating habits, positivity and the determination to succeed. You can go to your local bookstore (or a Barnes and Noble for a wider selection) and pick up books like The Kind Diet by Alicia Silverstone or The Ketogenic Diet by Lyle Mcdonald to help get you thinking about different types of nutritional diets and how they affect your body. Many attest to the benefits of a vegan diet – but you can also get some those benefits from limiting your meat and dairy intake on a daily basis too. Find ways to still reap the benefits of various diets without feeling deprived.

It might take a while before you fall in love with a "plan" and decide to stick to it, but the point is to get yourself thinking about what you eat every day and whether it's serving you. When in doubt, keep it simple: consume lots of greens and fruits, lean protein whenever possible, limit your sugar, dairy and salt intake and drink plenty of water every day. Soy and almond milk can be great replacements for milk or cream. If you're a caffeine junkie like I am, try to substitute coffee with some decaffeinated green tea to jumpstart your metabolism while still getting a dose of some healthy antioxidants. Ensure that you have variety on your plate so you don't get bored or fed up with eating the same old meal plan every day. Get creative. Maybe one day you'll have a delicious green juice along with a Caesar salad, but the next day you'll have some pasta with a variety of veggies and grilled chicken. Have FUN with your food – and relax. This is not about feeling guilty or ashamed about your food habits or diet. It's about eating more mindfully in a way that serves you – mind, body, and spirit.

This is also not about losing weight (although that may be one of your goals). It's about losing the negative health effects of eating an excess of things that don't serve you nutritionally and about adding healthier, balanced meals. Not only will it give you a sense of empowerment that you are treating your body well, it will give you the added benefit of a long-term healthy lifestyle and strengthened immune system that will not be easily conquered by stress.

Self-care for the body: my personal journey to eating mindfully. For me personally, small steps like reducing my meat, dairy and salt consumption, adding green tea (for antioxidants) and kale to my diet, replacing sugar with natural sweeteners, adding vegetables and fruits in a creative way to my meals (as smoothies, side dishes or cooking it as part of the entrée itself), drinking lemon water every morning to detoxify my body and replacing soda with water have all helped me create a healthier lifestyle in the long run. These steps have helped me to conquer physical illness as well by boosting my immune system.

Take the time to research what diet may be best for you and your body, as not every diet will be suitable for everyone. A more plant-based vegan diet was optimal for me and was one I felt was best for the environment, but the diet that may be best for you may look very different. Consulting a nutritionist as well as your primary doctor, reading books on nutrition, exploring both traditional as well as natural remedies and conducting some research on what types of food best suit you and your particular ailments can do wonders not only for your self-care but your sense of agency and power.

Never "shame" yourself for having a day where you treat yourself or feeling as if you're not meeting your fitness goals fast enough– in fact, have at least one day a week where you do treat yourself so you're not feeling like you're sacrificing the pleasures of life just to fit society's expectations. Stress only heightens cortisol levels which actually contributes to our bodies not feeling well or fit. Enjoying a little cake on the weekends or having a glass of wine once in a while isn't the end of the world – it's all about moderation. Balance your decadence with your due diligence – in a guilt-free manner – and you will find it actually accelerates your journey towards your best self.

The benefits of exercise and a clean diet come naturally when we show ourselves self-compassion along with our goal-setting. When we treat our bodies as sacred, we reap the benefits. When we honor our bodies and love our bodies, we strengthen our resolve to bring them back to their optimal state. And when we practice nonjudgment, we allow ourselves to move towards our goals while still remaining gentle towards ourselves.

Counseling can be an incredibly effective resource for someone dealing with chronic loneliness, depression, anxiety and/or the effects of trauma. Depending on your financial situation, you may be eligible to receive counseling on a low-cost basis. If you're enrolled in college, it may also be included with your student health plan. Most colleges have some sort of counseling or wellness center that also provide crisis-based, short- term counseling to aid you during a difficult time. Take advantage of any university or community resources available to you: your mental health will thank you.

Encourage yourself to do some research on the resources available to you in your area. Do not believe in the stigma about seeing a therapist; it takes a strong person to seek out help and resources. Anyone who tells you differently is not in touch with his or her mental health or self-care. Asking for help with your mental health is not only your right, it's your duty to yourself. Also, don't settle for a therapist who doesn't meet your needs or is not compatible with you.

Remember: there are many therapists who aren't going to meet your needs. You might need a particular type of therapist who specializes in treatments like Cognitive Behavioral Therapy or Dialectical Behavioral Therapy depending on your specific issues. Cognitive Behavioral Therapy is excellent for arming yourself against irrational thoughts and cognitive distortions. It will eventually also help you to improve the negative behaviors and habits you actively engaged in based on these irrational thoughts.

On the other hand, Dialectical Behavioral Therapy is ideal for someone who wants to benefit from mindfulness techniques and gain more knowledge about emotion regulation, distress tolerance and interpersonal effectiveness. If you're dealing with more specific issues like bulimia and anorexia, substance abuse or other addictions, you will need to do research and find a therapist who specializes in these issues.

Or you might struggle with specific disorders such as OCD and need someone who's experienced in exposure therapy. Maybe you suffer from PTSD and need a trauma-informed therapist who is experienced in treating patients with the effects of trauma. Make sure you do your research (start with a simple Google search) on what type of therapy might suit you best before you settle for the most basic talk therapy you can afford; the Psychology Today website has a search engine where you can track down both group support and individual therapists depending on your area. For many people, talk therapy is extremely helpful in talking about present-day issues but it doesn't always enable you to effectively and holistically address the ingrained patterns and habits that you need to break with specific techniques. So don't be afraid to branch out and research different types of therapies or techniques – whether it's EMDR, EFT, hypnotherapy or even art therapy – the sky's the limit.

The style of your therapist is also important. You might find the seemingly perfect therapist (low-cost, specializes in something you need) and still find yourself feeling more enraged, hurt or invalidated in some way during the therapeutic process. This is because therapists range in personality, demeanor and approach. That's why it is important to find someone who will simultaneously provide a validating environment while still enabling you to challenge yourself in productive ways.

It is also important that you also remember there are cultural limitations to interactions between clients and therapists who come from differing cultures. Not every therapist will understand the specific cultural background you come from, so it's important to find one who is multiculturally competent and able to assist you in culturally-sensitive ways.

Therapy is meant to be challenging and difficult because you are addressing problems you may have repressed for a long time. However, if you can't even communicate openly with your current therapist, there is a problem. Lines of communication disrupt the productive mediation of issues and interfere with the therapeutic alliance that preserves trust and collaboration in the relationship.

This is a hindrance to your recovery and must be addressed. Do you have a tough love therapist who always seems to judge you through his tone and gestures?

What about the therapist who falls asleep just while listening to you? Or maybe you have a less expressive therapist who nods and says "Mmmhmm," to everything. If this happens a lot, do you wonder if it would've made a difference if you had enlisted a wall to talk to rather than a licensed professional?

Many people struggle with ending a relationship with a therapist even when this person is unable to meet their needs. This is often mirrored in the way they deal with other interpersonal relationships which they also feel powerless to end. Make sure you are getting the care you need from a professional who really does have what it takes to meet your needs. Like any friendship or relationship, you have to evaluate whether or not this person is worthy of playing such an important role in your self-care regimen.

HELPFUL ONLINE RESOURCES AND TOOLS

Baggage Reclaim Blog by Natalie Lue:
http://baggagereclaim.com/

Getting Past Your Breakup Blog by Susan Elliot
http://www.gettingpastyourbreakup.com/
gettingpastyourpast

Good Vibe Blog
http://www.goodvibeblog.com

Yoga for Beginners
http://www.yogabasics.com/practice/yoga-for-
beginners/

Meetup
http://www.meetup.com/

Meditating for Beginners:
http://www.how-to-meditate.org/breathing-
meditations.htm/

Meditation Oasis by Richard and Mary Maddox
http://www.meditationoasis.com/podcast/

Calming Corner Meditation MP3s (NYU)
https://www.nyu.edu/life/safety-health-wellness/student-health-center/services/mental-health/relaxation-oasis/calming-corner.html

Free Meditation and Spirituality Podcasts:
http://meditation.org.au/podcast_directory.asp

Michael Sealey's YouTube Channel
https://www.youtube.com/user/MichaelSealey

CBT Skills Handouts
http://www.morninglightcounseling.org/healing-a-recovery/67-tools-for-recovery/132-handouts-on-cbt-skills

Psychology Today – Therapist Search Engine
http://www.therapists.psychologytoday.com

DBT Skills
http://dbtselfhelp.com/index.html

Nutrition Blog Network
http://www.nutritionblognetwork.com/

Practical Wisdom for Clarity, Freedom and Happiness blog by Gail Brenner
http://gailbrenner.com/

Art Therapy and Trauma
http://www.internationalarttherapy.org/trauma.html

3 STOP BEING A PEOPLE-PLEASER

AND START BEING YOUR AUTHENTIC SELF

Minimizing behavior that pleases others more than you is an essential component of becoming your authentic self. When you embrace and validate your own thoughts, feelings, values, boundaries, past experiences, and future goals without having to please people, you come that much closer to simply being you and living a life that accurately reflects what you want, need and deserve. For young women who grow up in environments where being complaint is habitual and necessary to get their basic needs met, people-pleasing can be a difficult and toxic habit to overcome. Studies demonstrate that an early invalidating family environment can interact with the biological vulnerabilities of children to produce various forms of psychopathology and emotional regulation deficiencies (Haslam, Mountford, Meyer and Waller, 2008; Crowell, Beauchaine, and Linehan, 2009).

Even for children who do not have biological vulnerabilities or predispositions towards psychopathology, traumatic environments breed toxic interpersonal and maladaptive emotion regulation skills. These habits become even more pronounced in a world where young women also have to struggle with rampant inequalities such as rape culture, street harassment and domestic violence.

HOW DO YOU KNOW YOU'RE A PEOPLE-PLEASER?

This chapter is especially helpful for those who are chronic people-pleasers.

Symptoms include but are not limited to: saying yes when you really mean no, allowing people to trample all over your boundaries on a weekly basis without asserting yourself, and "performing" character traits or behaviors that do not speak to your authentic self. Can cause high blood pressure and stewing resentment that festers for years until the "last straw," at which point, sounds of an explosion erupt. You're so tired of being Jekyll all the time you become the worst version of Hyde possible to let out all the steam that was simmering within all along.

Jokes aside, people-pleasing is becoming a sad epidemic in our lives, and it's not just restricted to peer pressure among teenagers. We've all done it at some point, and some amount of people-pleasing might even be necessary in contexts like the workplace. However, people-pleasing can be a difficult habit to eradicate if being compliant is something we've been taught is necessary to avoid conflict. Think of children who grow up in abusive households: if they're taught that whenever they displease authority figures they will be punished just for being themselves, they may be subconsciously programmed to navigate conflict similarly when it comes to future interpersonal relationships.

PEOPLE-PLEASING, ABUSE AND SELF-CARE

Adults can engage in people-pleasing to an unhealthy extent, to the point where they engage in friendships and relationships that don't serve their needs, fail to walk away from toxic situations, and put on a "persona" rather than donning their true selves because they are afraid of what people will think of them. This can keep us in overdrive to meet the needs and wants of others, while failing to serve our own needs and wants. People-pleasing essentially deprives of us of the ability and the right to engage in healthy self-care.

People-pleasing of course becomes more complex in the context of abusive relationships where the dynamics are so toxic that it's difficult for survivors to simply walk away when faced with cognitive dissonance, Stockholm syndrome and gaslighting (you can learn more about these in Chapter Five). At this point, it's no longer just people-pleasing but the misfortune of being caught in the midst of a vicious abuse cycle.

However, people-pleasing does make it easier to ignore red flags of abusive relationships at the very early stages especially with covert manipulators. We can also become conditioned to continually "please" if we're used to walking on eggshells around our abuser. This is why knowing our own boundaries and values is extremely important in order to protect ourselves and listen to our intuition, especially when it's screaming loudly at us. Minimizing people- pleasing is also vital in the process of going No Contact with our abusers.

WHAT CAUSES PEOPLE-PLEASING?

A toxic environment that promotes submissive compliance and enables other unhealthy behavior can be described by the following:

A family dynamic where verbal or physical abuse is present or where basic needs are always being negotiated or challenged can cultivate a fear of retaliation which ultimately holds people back from being their true selves.

Being constantly browbeaten or silenced for having your own opinions or expressing your emotions in a romantic relationship, friendship or familial relationship. This involves repeated invalidation of your thoughts, feelings and experiences by an abusive partner, friend or caretaker. "Gaslighting" is a phrase used to describe a tactic employed by an abuser who makes you doubt the accuracy of your own realities. For example, an abuser may pretend that you are crazy and deny the reality of his or her actions when you bring up something he or she did wrong.

Childhood trauma or trauma in adolescence. Examples include bullying, sexual assault, witnessing a traumatic event or experiencing loss or abandonment. These traumas can shape early brain development and interfere with effective interpersonal habits or coping methods. We can easily become conditioned by these traumas to feel powerless and unable to exercise our agency to influence the environment which can appear as a consistent source of hostility or degradation. We also internalize these experiences as a reflection of our own unworthiness or incompetence.

Overcoming such negative past experiences and the impact they have on your self-esteem takes a great deal of work and time, but there are some techniques that can be employed every day to "disarm" the toxicity of these experiences and reduce the urge to please people at the expense of your own needs and wants.

Part of healing is reframing the way we think about pleasing others versus pleasing ourselves. Here's a revolutionary thought: what if I told you that your needs and wants were just as important as the people you were desperately trying to please, if not more? What if I claimed that your entire existence - your goals, your dreams, your feelings, your thoughts were in some way valid and needed to be addressed? Just as valid as the friend you're trying to impress or the parent whose approval you seek?

PEOPLE-PLEASING AND ITS RELATIONSHIP TO REJECTION

We all seek approval at times and many of us fear rejection if we dare to show our authentic selves. By trying so hard to avoid rejection, we end up rejecting ourselves. The problem arises when this becomes a consistent habit and leaves us vulnerable to manipulation, exploitation and dependency on others for our sense of self-worth. When you're not honoring your authentic self, you're depriving others of the chance to see the real you, the right to judge you on your own merits and not the persona you perform.

Remember that rule on airplanes about parents putting on their oxygen masks before they put the oxygen mask on their children? Well there's a simple reason for that - we have to take care of ourselves first before we can take care of others. If we exhaust our own reserves to the point where we have nothing left, we won't be helping others at all.

The first step to minimize people-pleasing is to radically accept the realities of how inevitable rejection is. We cannot and should not try to please everyone. Some people will like you. Some people will dislike you. Others will outright hate you for their own reasons and preferences. And guess what? That's okay. You have the right to do it too. You don't have to like everyone or approve of everyone either. You have your own preferences, judgments, biases, feelings and opinions of others too. Don't be afraid of that, and don't fear rejection. Instead, reject the rejecter and move forward with your life.

You cannot let people-pleasing detract from the real you - by working so hard to gain the approval of others, you inevitably risk losing yourself. You become a puppet led by the needs and wants of various puppeteers. In the most extreme cases, people-pleasing can cost you your mental health and years off of your life. So stop cheerleading bad behavior and start cultivating your authentic self!

TOOLS TO MINIMIZE PEOPLE-PLEASING

Establish your core boundaries and values in interpersonal relationships. Start to minimize people-pleasing today by getting together a list of your top boundaries and values which you will not allow anyone to trespass in intimate relationships or friendships.

After crafting this list, you can create a boundaries worksheet to write down ways in which your boundaries have been crossed in the past and the actions you can take to protect your boundaries in the future.

For example, my boundaries and values list might include things like:

I will not accept being spoken to in a condescending or rude manner by my friends, family members or relationship partners.

I will not tolerate any physical aggression or physical threats from anyone.

I value honesty, respect and emotional validation in all of my friendships and relationships.

I require that my partner respect my views even if he or she doesn't agree with them.

If a friend or partner wants to get together with me, he or she must schedule it in advance and not request to meet with me last minute.

For each of these boundaries, you can then list a time when this boundary was trespassed and then the action you will take in the future to protect that boundary. For example:

BOUNDARY TRESPASSED: My friend asked me to come to a movie last minute because her other friend canceled on her. I didn't want to disappoint her, so I went, even though I had to stop working on my essay to do it.

FUTURE ACTION: The next time my friend asks me to drop something last minute to accommodate spontaneous plans with her, I'll let her know that I have other plans and that I can't.

BOUNDARY TRESPASSED: My relative keeps leaving me voicemail messages that border on abusive whenever I don't respond to her right away.

FUTURE ACTION: The next time she leaves me a voicemail like that, I will call her and firmly let her know that the way she is speaking to me is not OK. If she still continues to do this, I will either delete her voicemail messages without listening to them or block her number altogether.

Do many of these before you get a grip on which boundaries you want to protect in the future. Your specific boundaries or values will depend on your own personal experiences, needs, wants and beliefs. Some boundaries are absolutely necessary and central to our self-care (such as boundaries that protect you from tolerating verbal, emotional and physical abuse), while others are more tailored to our specific desires of how we wish to be treated.

Positive self-affirmations or mantras. These are phrases or words you can repeat to yourself to reinforce the behaviors and thought patterns you wish to cultivate, phrases such as, "I am a happy person," "I love myself," or "I am successful." Not only do these phrases eventually become ingrained in the subconscious and positively affect our behavior, positive affirmations also do the extremely important work of replacing or at least leaving less room for the negative abusive phrases you may have experienced in the past.

Creating "lists" or "manifestos" of reference that challenge your usual negative thought patterns. It could be a list of accomplishments and aspirations for the future. It could be a list of all the compliments you've ever received. It could even be a few sentences telling you that you will make it through any obstacle. Or, it could be pages worth about the type of person you are and all the great things about you. The point of it is having a physical document that you can refer to in times of duress, doubt or anxiety which will redirect you in a positive direction rather than dragging you down the usual derogatory path of self-destruction.

Crafting a reverse discourse. "Reverse discourse" isn't something I necessarily learned in a psychology book or a therapeutic program. It's a series of techniques I taught
myself to decrease negative ruminations. In the work of Foucault, reverse discourse was discussed as a medium through which power was reclaimed and redirected. In the way I am using it (or adapting it), creating a reverse discourse involves a reclaiming of power, connotation and values of negative statements wielded at you by toxic people over your lifetime.

Many people use reverse discourse in contemporary culture to reclaim derogatory names or slurs. For example, the international movement "Slutwalk" was one that sought to reclaim the demonizing power of the word "slut" which has been historically used to control female sexuality. Individuals in this movement reclaimed this word and marched against rape culture. This rape culture encouraged using the word "slut" to transfer the responsibility of rape from a perpetrator's actions to a victim's manner of dress or behavior. In the framework of emotional abuse and bullying, there are multiple ways to create an empowering reverse discourse. Here are some ideas:

Craft a creative and strategic response you can use for any rumination. Did someone call you "ugly" or "stupid" in the past? Can you think of comebacks to these claims? List them and remember the items from this list or pull it out whenever you find yourself ruminating over harsh words. What may seem like a silly exercise is actually one of the first steps to empowering you to "talk back" to the bullies you never had a chance to talk back to.

For example, if I was remembering a time when someone called me ugly, one of my "comebacks" might be, "They must be looking at themselves in the mirror. Only ugly people see ugliness in others, after all." Your reverse discourse doesn't have to be a sentence or paragraph long. It doesn't even have to be particularly clever. It just has to be empowering enough for you to stop the negative rumination in its tracks and return the flow of power to a more positive evaluation of yourself.

Reclaim the terminology of words by reviving it with creative, positive meaning. If you feel up to it, you may even use the term given to you as an empowering term. For example, if someone says, "You're grief," you might note, "I am proud to be a source of grief to weak people," and remember this whenever rumination of this negative phrase comes up.

Essentially, you're telling yourself that what this person told you was a flaw is actually a strength in disguise. Being an annoyance to people who do cannot "tolerate" fulfilling your emotional needs is actually a blessing, not a curse. This might not work for all words – it is important that while attempting this you do not accidentally internalize the negative essence of the word you are using. Try using it as part of a mantra in order to recondition this word as an empowering, rather than degrading tool.

Replace the word. This is creating a complete reversal. Whenever negative words or phrases from your past rear their ugly heads, replace words like "ugly" or "brain dead" with "beautiful" and "brilliant." Again, using these as protective mantras whenever negative cognitions come up will help work with your unconscious to associate your self-image with more positive attributions.

Challenge the power and meaning of these words. Challenging the value of these negative words can also be accomplished by writing down the positive feedback others have given you, to counter snide remarks or abusive comments that you find yourself ruminating over.

Whether you choose to create lists that outright challenge all the negative declarations toxic people have made about you or create rapid responses to every day ruminations, creating this reverse discourse is necessary to remembering that your self-worth and identity are not equivalent to the abuse you received. Remember that bullies and abusers see the light and beauty in someone and always try to snuff it out. Don't let them win.

You're beautiful, precious and worthy. Your life and worth is not defined by someone else's opinions of you, especially since these are often projected insecurities of the bullies or abusers themselves. Unless they're providing compassionate constructive criticism, naysayers have no say in your worth or abilities. They usually nitpick others who have accomplished more than they could ever have the courage to achieve. Use their doubt to fuel your motivation for success and self-love. Constructing these responses are necessary to revising the script others have written for you, and staging your own recovery by rewriting yourself.

Use your imperfections and flaws to advance your purpose. Sometimes your biggest weaknesses can be transformed into your greatest strengths. For example, I've always been told by people that I am too sensitive. The people around me have always seen this as a flaw, but I've turned it into my strength. My sensitivity may be a shortcoming in some situations, but it is also one of my greatest strengths, because it gives me the ability to empathize with people and have compassion for them on a deeper level. It is what helped me write this book and what makes my work as a mental health advocate so rewarding. Understand both your strengths and so-called weaknesses and how they make you beautifully, uniquely you.

Instead of attempting to erase your authentic self or reach perfection, see how your flaws can be used to serve your personal purpose. For example, if your flaw is that you are a very stubborn person, you may want to reevaluate how you can channel this stubbornness into productive outlets – for example, using your stubbornness to devote yourself to social justice issues and stand up for the underdog. This doesn't mean we don't strive towards self-improvement where self-improvement is warranted; it just means we place flaws and shortcomings in the framework of personal growth.

Be bold every day. It may take some baby steps before you start challenging the status quo. So if you're just starting out, commit yourself to one more bold action of self-love EACH day. That means every day, you do something that expresses the authentic you. It can be big or small, but it has to be something that authentically expresses your needs, wants, values and preferences. For example, one day you may choose to wear an outfit simply because you like it, not because you're trying to impress anyone. Another day, you may choose to turn down an invitation to go out because you really need rest. You may eventually progress to the point where this becomes a habit in your everyday relationships – expressing your dissatisfaction, asserting what you truly think, and making it known to others what your boundaries are and what makes you comfortable. Whatever you do, make sure it's for your own BENEFIT and does not stem from your need to please or coddle and serve others. That is key.

Develop a healthier relationship with rejection. Rejection hurts, but what hurts even more is debasing yourself and your self-respect for the sake of maintaining a toxic relationship or friendship. Rejection can send us spinning in ruminations over our self-worth and desirability. Whether you were rejected from a job, within a relationship, a potential romance, or a friendship, rejection can threaten our sense of self-efficacy, self-image and self- esteem if we don't learn to embrace and cope with it in healthier ways. Rejection can also maximize people- pleasing because we may feel like we are at fault for it and must try harder to win someone else's approval.

Here are some crucial ways we can develop a healthier relationship with rejection and cope with it in productive ways. I call it the "Three R's of Coping with Rejection."

The Three R's: Challenge the Rumination, Redirection to Something Better and Rejuvenating a Sense of Self

1. Challenge the Rumination

Challenge your irrational thoughts and beliefs. Rejection makes us vulnerable to cognitive distortions, inaccurate thoughts or beliefs that perpetuate negative emotions. When we feel rejected by others, we may engage in "Black and White" distortions where we perceive ourselves or the situation as "all bad" or "all good." We may also participate in filtering,where we exclusively focus on the negative details of an event rather than the positive ones. Most likely, rejection will lead to some amount of personalization where we attribute the blame of someone else's negative toxic behavior to ourselves, as well as overgeneralization, where we interpret that one event of rejection as evidence for a never-ending pattern unlikely to change.

What do you think happens when you carry around these false beliefs? Most likely, you end up with a partial or full-on self- fulfilling prophecy, because cognitive distortions tend to affect our perceived agency in navigating constraints and opportunities in our daily lives. If we think we can't do it, we often don't even bother trying - we don't get the job because we don't believe we're qualified to even apply for it. We don't achieve healthy relationships if we believe we're not good enough. We may end up having a never-ending pattern of bad luck in relationships because we sabotage ourselves in ways we may not even be aware of and maintain connections with toxic partners. Rejection can prompt us reject ourselves under these false assumptions and subsequent actions.

Try this exercise. Start by writing down a list of ten negative, false beliefs you hold about yourself, the power of rejection, and its connection to your perceived self-worth. These can include beliefs like, "Rejection means I am a bad person," "If someone rejects me, it means I am not good enough," or "I need people's approval before I can approve of myself."

Next, write down ten reevaluations next to these beliefs. These include thoughts that challenge the beliefs or provide evidence against it, like, "Rejection is about the other person's expectations and preferences, not about my worth as a person," or "I can feel good about myself regardless of someone else's perception of me." If it proves helpful, try to think of examples where these challenges were true. For example, you might think about how someone else's expectations for a relationship differed from your own and shaped his or her rejection of you (or more accurately, the relationship itself).

Or, more importantly, you might remember a time when you yourself rejected someone, not because of his or worth, but because of your own needs, wants and preferences. Putting yourself in the rejecter's place enables you to gain a broader perspective that resists personalizing the rejection and helps you to move forward. You're essentially reminding yourself that everyone, at some point, gets rejected by something or someone, and it's not an experience exclusive to you or indicative of how much you're worth.

2. Redirection to Something Better

Rejection doesn't have to be a negative thing - it can be a positive release of your efforts, and a redirection towards something or someone more worthy of you. What are the ways this specific rejection has freed you? Have you gotten laid off from a job and now have the opportunity to work on your true passion? Has the ending of a relationship enabled you to take care of yourself more fully and opened up time and space for friendship, travel, and new career prospects?

For every rejection, make a list of new opportunities and prospects that were not available to you prior to the rejection. Whether they be grandiose fantasies of what could be or more realistic goals, this will help train your mind into thinking of the infinite possibilities that have multiplied as a result of your rejection, rather than the limiting of possibilities we usually associate with the likes of rejection.

3. Rejuvenation of the Self

Remember that there is only one you and that a rejection of your uniqueness is a loss on the part of the rejector. We've heard this phrase, "there is only one you," time and time again but what does it really mean? It means that your specific package - quirks, personality, looks, talents, dreams, passions, flaws - can never be completely duplicated in another person. You are unique and possess a certain mixture of qualities no one else on this earth will ever be able to replicate even if they wanted to.

Embracing our uniqueness, while depersonalizing rejection, enables us to remember that rejection can be a redirection to something or someone better who can appreciate us fully. Whoever rejected you has ultimately lost out on your uniqueness - they will never again find someone exactly like you who acts the way you do and who makes them feel exactly the way you did. But guess what? It means someone else will. Another company will benefit from your hard work, perseverance, and talent. Another partner will enjoy the beautiful qualities that make you the unique person you are - your sense of humor, your intelligence and charisma. Another friend will be strengthened by your wisdom and compassion.

You are a gem and you don't have to waste your precious time attempting to morph yourself into anything else but you just to get someone to "approve" of your unique brand. You are who you are for a reason and you have a destiny to fulfill. Don't let rejection detract from that destiny. Let it redirect you to better things, remind you of how special you truly are and rejuvenate your sense of self rather than destroy it.

If you are the type of person who feels guilty about not pleasing people, then consider this:

There are many people living in the world that bust your boundaries but protect their own boundaries with fierce devotion. Recognize that this hypocrisy and double standard leaves you exploited and malnourished while others reap the benefits of your boundary-breaking compliance. Do you recall the times when someone expressed their dissatisfaction with you, or attempted to guilt-trip you into doing something? Or when someone outright disagreed with you without even considering your point of view? How come they get to say what they want and feel while you stifle your own thoughts? No one has the right to disrespect you, but plenty of people get away with doing so because you allow them to walk all over you and don't speak up for yourself. Do you really want to be a doormat while other people get what they need, want and deserve? Don't you also want to have your own desires heard and met?

You can still learn from these toxic people by maintaining a delicate balance: asserting your needs with respect, but with conviction. Don't be afraid to back up your decisions, your assertions and your opinions with your actions. Don't back down, but always remember that maximizing the power of your authentic self gives you the power to finally walk away from people who aren't prepared to give you what you need and deserve. Recognizing all of this and reevaluating your unhealthy habits to please people is extremely important to having a healthy self-esteem. All of these techniques are there to help you realize that you are important, valuable and you deserve to have your voice heard.

Also remember to use your voice to make a positive change in the lives of others. Standing up for yourself also means you can stand up for others. If you know someone who is being bullied and abused, speak out. Don't be afraid to stand up on their behalf. Thinking "I won't pick sides" in the battle between good and evil is one of the most dangerous things you can ever do. Use your voice to shatter the silence that hides and perpetuates violence.

Minimizing people-pleasing behavior will return the power back to you, and enable you to pursue what you truly desire. What's holding you back from accomplishing your deepest dreams and pursuing your true passion? Is it shame, guilt, fear, insecurity? Is it pressures from society? Whatever is holding you back, let it go. You are who you are for a reason. You were meant to live that dream and change the world in your own, unique way. You were meant to be a leader, but you can't be a leader if you remain a follower. Don't sell the real you short by pretending to be someone else or following someone else's path for you. Own your own story and inspire others in the process. Embrace your authentic you and you will come that much closer to accomplishing your dreams.

HELPFUL ONLINE RESOURCES AND TOOLS

Drawing Effective Personal Boundaries Worksheet:
http://www.liveandworkonpurpose.com/files/Boundaries.pdf

21 Tips to Stop Being a People-Pleaser
http://psychcentral.com/lib/21-tips-to-stop-being-a-people- pleaser/0007158

10 Ways to Say No from The Society of Recovering Doormats
http://thesocietyforrecoveringdoormats.com/2014/08/10/10-ways- to-say-no/

12 Core Boundaries to Live by in Dating and Relationships
http://www.baggagereclaim.co.uk/12-core-boundaries-to-live-by-in-life-dating-relationships/

Five Ways to Build Healthy Boundaries
http://www.writingthroughlife.com/five-ways-to-build-healthy- boundaries

Different Types of Personal Boundaries
http://psychcentral.com/lib/what-are-personal-
boundaries-how-do- i-get-some/00016100

10 Ways to Practice Positive Rebellion
http://allisoncrow.com/10-ways-to-practice-positive-
rebellion/

DBT Interpersonal Effectiveness Handout:
http://www.dbtselfhelp.com/html/ie_handout_8.html

Healthy Boundaries Information Sheet:
http://ehcounseling.com/materials/boundaries_2
006_06_06.pdf

Codependency Book List by the Guru Herself, Melody Beattie
http://melodybeattie.com/codependency/

4 MINDFULNESS AND YOUR SELF-CARE TOOLKIT

During stressful times, we may get so distracted by our strife that we struggle to enjoy the happy moments that make our lives meaningful. Mindfulness, which involves turning our attention back to the present moment, is essential to refocusing our mind, body and spirit from the past and placing it solidly into the reality of the here and now.

There are many diverse ways to define mindfulness and there are different practices associated with mindfulness across Western and Eastern traditions. To keep things simple, I'll be sticking to mindfulness as a mechanism for emotion regulation, attentiveness and acceptance of the present moment by discussing how it is used in the framework of dialectical behavioral therapy (DBT). Although DBT is usually used for specific populations who have trouble regulating their emotions, I find that the skill set it teaches can be applicable to anyone and everyone looking to become more mindful in life and can even help those who struggle with symptoms of PTSD or Complex PTSD caused by chronic trauma.

DBT teaches skills related to four modules: core mindfulness, distress tolerance, interpersonal effectiveness and emotion regulation (McKay, Wood and Brantley 2007). All of these skills are interconnected and interact with one another; learning mindfulness skills for example, helps with distress tolerance, interpersonal effectiveness and emotion regulation.

In DBT, the mindfulness module is used to teach patients how to observe the present moment, learn how to describe it effectively and participate in the present moment nonjudgmentally. We are able to use "grounding" techniques to situate ourselves in the here and now. This is done in the following ways:

1. Observing – "Generally, the ability to attend to events requires the ability to step back from the event itself" (DBTSelfHelp). Observing mindfully means paying attention to events, emotions and other behavioral responses by allowing us to experience the present moment with complete awareness of what's occurring, in our environment and within ourselves, without attempting to necessarily act.

2. Describing – In order to observe the present moment effectively, we can ground ourselves in the present by describing to ourselves what is happening. If we're taking a shower, for example, we might notice the feeling of the soap on our skin, the aroma of our shampoo, and the temperature of the water. This "locks" us into the present moment and helps us resist becoming easily distracted. We can also use these describing skills to articulate our emotions more effectively and pinpoint why we may be feeling the way we do. For example, when we're angry, rather than being reactive, we might describe our state as, "My face is flushed. My hands are sweaty. My heart is racing. I feel a tightness in my chest," which enables us to look at our emotional state and the bodily sensations that accompany it more objectively.

3. Participating – This is where we can really test our observing and describing skills by engaging with the moment fully and participating in it with comprehensive awareness. If we're in the classroom, we might participate actively by listening attentively to the professor, noticing the students around us, and being aware of our own body, thoughts and feelings. This means engaging without judging, observing without ruminating. Being in the moment requires our full attention, so even noticing every object that is a certain color is a way we're forced to participate and engage fully with the present moment without being too self-conscious. It's all about maintaining an awareness of self and environment simultaneously, and engaging our attention fully with everything around us.

All three requires us to abide by the following principles:

Nonjudgment – All of the above skills should be attempted with a nonjudgmental stance. Since we are conditioned to place judgments on our observations, taking this stance means we can notice what's occurring with a sense of gentleness and willingness to let go. This means not prolonging a thought or emotion when it occurs. It means that when we notice threatening stimuli, we decouple our immediate emotional reaction from our behavioral response. We learn to approach seemingly hostile or threatening situations in a more accepting manner. This can help us save energy in our responses to situations and as an added bonus, can also enhance the quality of our interpersonal relationships because we're required to step back and not judge others based on just how we feel at the moment.

One thing at a time mindfully – To focus our attention properly, it's helpful to try to focus exclusively on one activity at a time so that specific activity has our full engagement. When we're talking with a friend, we're engaging with them fully and not checking our cell phone. When we're eating mindfully, we're savoring the scents and tastes of our food and not attempting to read or watch television at the same time. When we're meditating, we're meditating and not trying to solve problems. Doing one thing at a time helps us to zero in our focus into the present moment and not be distracted by the other tasks we have to do. It also saves important emotional reserves because we only invest time and energy into one activity at a time.

Effectiveness – This skill is most related to the end result of radical acceptance. When we're focusing on doing what is effective rather than what we perceive to be "right" or "wrong" or "fair" or unfair," we avoid passing a moral judgment which might actually encourage maladaptive responses to life's everyday situations. For example, if I encounter a mentally ill person on the street who yells at me (quite a frequent occurrence in the streets of New York), I can feel defensive and angry, or I can act mindfully and effectively by choosing to take a breath, cross the street and avoid what might become a dangerous, violent or tumultuous situation. In acting effectively and mindfully rather than reactively or judgmentally, I can skillfully navigate situations with an increased sense of awareness, acceptance and agency (McKay, Wood and Brantley, 2007).

You might be thinking, this looks easy enough. So why do I have so much trouble practicing mindfulness even though I agree with the value of all its underlying concepts? Four significant factors contribute to our feeling of stress and detract from our ability to feel joy fully and with mindfulness:

1. Resistance to the Present Moment - Due to anger, anxiety or discomfort, our thoughts often replay stressful events and continue the vicious cycle of unhappiness. Even if we are in a different setting, context and have the means to enjoy the present moment, we struggle to do so. In order to reduce this form of resistance, you have to be willing to stop being resistant to your own emotions. You don't have to "force" yourself to feel differently – approach each emotion with an attitude of, "Each emotion is telling me something. Each emotion has value. If I am angry, it's for a reason. I can feel free to feel my anger without acting upon it. I can process it, honor it, understand it, validate it. I can find the pain beneath the surface level emotion. And by doing so, I can heal."

2. Obsessive, ruminating thoughts - Very much related to the lack of mindfulness above, ruminating thoughts regenerate the feeling that the same stressful event is happening to us again, and our brain finds it difficult to distinguish the present moment from the past. Intrusive thoughts, flashbacks or nightmares can also be a sign of PTSD or acute stress disorder from the trauma we have experienced. In what is known as an "emotional flashback," we regress back into a childlike state of helplessness and pervasive worthlessness, similar to what we may have experienced in childhood or early adolescence. Remember that trauma and the memories of what trauma felt like is also stored in our bodies (Van der Kolk, 2014). It is helpful to always see a trauma therapist when trying out new ways to cope with ruminating thoughts. You can also use grounding techniques like those involved in yoga or meditation to help to slow down some of the ruminations that are occurring.

3. Physical discomfort caused by anxiety – Anxiety increases physical tension in our bodies which in turn increases our feeling of overall emotional unease. If we don't learn how to manage our anxiety in healthier ways, we are left paralyzed during Fight or Flight mode. It's a negative feedback loop that goes on forever: our bodies tense in response to the emotion, we interpret this physiological arousal in catastrophic ways, and this confirms our interpretation that something is indeed very wrong, validating the fears behind our anxiety and our seeming inability to cope with it. In order to interrupt the cycle at its wake, it can be helpful to verbalize what we are experiencing. According to trauma therapist Pete Walker (2013), even just saying something like, "I am having an emotional flashback" can help to interrupt our free-fall into anxiety.

4. Inactivity and Lack of Positive Reinforcement from the Environment – A psychologist by the name of Lewinsohn theorized that depression was caused by a loss of positive reinforcement from the environment (Alloy et. al, 2005). If we experience losses or lack consistent activities that reward our efforts, we feel unwilling to make any efforts. With a lack of distraction, supportive communities or hobbies we enjoy, we find it difficult to be engaged and active in life. In turn, we become physically and emotionally sluggish, perpetuating the idea that enjoyment in life is impossible to obtain. We suffer from what is known as anhedonia, a lack of pleasure in the activities we used to enjoy.

To counteract these negative effects, there are some useful techniques to enhance mindfulness, our experience of joy or to create a feeling of joy:

Radical acceptance – Radical acceptance is the act of accepting the present circumstances just as they are, without resistance. This acknowledges that our resistance to the present moment actually exacerbates rather than improves our suffering. Radical acceptance does not mean we accept abuse or mistreatment. On the contrary, in circumstances where we can make positive changes and keep ourselves out of harm's way, we should acknowledge that agency and be proactive.

However, radical acceptance cultivates a resilience towards events from our past and present which we can no longer control, such as a past filled with abuse and disrespect, and acknowledges that we can live and thrive despite the pain we've suffered. Radical acceptance also does not mean we absolve others of their responsibility for their actions. We can accept things the way they are without necessarily condoning the harmful actions of others. We are simply letting go of the need to control things we cannot change – events that have already occurred or the actions of other people. With minimal resistance, we open ourselves up to the possibility of regaining control over the one thing we can change – ourselves. In order to effectively practice radical acceptance, we must first start with meditations that ease us into a sense of openness and willingness to accept things just as they are in the present moment, before we move onto radically accepting what we can or cannot change in our lives.

Radical Acceptance requires accepting the following principles:

1. Accepting reality for what it is, not what you want it to be. This is helpful to curb denial and to prevent ourselves from having judgments about situations or our emotions which can add onto stress. We deal with situations only as they are, and don't waste our energy on wishful thinking.

2. Accepting that the event or situation causing you pain has a cause. This principle allows us to look at situations without moral judgment and accept that every event had some sort of cause. Rather than trying to resist emotionally and say, "It shouldn't be like this," which leads to excess sadness and anger about the situation, we willingly accept that there is a reason behind what happened, even if we don't know what the reason is.

However, this doesn't mean you automatically blame yourself. The reason may very well be that something terrible happened to us due to the cruel actions of a person with less empathy and compassion than us – if you have been abused or assaulted, the fault lies 100% with the perpetrator.

3. Accepting that life can be worth living even with the existence of painful events. This principle enables us to recognize that life is still worth living despite our obstacles and adversity, which builds emotional resilience. The acceptance of this principle allows an individual to cope adaptively rather than maladaptively (such as through self-harm or other destructive behaviors) to overwhelming feelings of pain.

Create a consistent schedule of pleasurable, rewarding activities – For the following weeks, try this experiment. Write down a schedule of daily activities, with at least two pleasurable activities each day. For example, on Tuesdays, you may schedule watching your favorite television show or reading a book. On Wednesdays you might go to yoga and write. What's important is that the schedule is consistent, pleasurable and accessible for you.

Engaging in a schedule of daily activities rewards our Behavioral Activation System (BAS), our internal goal- directed motivation system which relies on cues associated with rewards from the environment (Alloy et. al, 2005). The more we feed this system, the happier and more positive we're bound to feel. With this consistent schedule,we are essentially countering the stagnation often associated with the loss of positive reinforcement from the environment.

Opposite Action - This technique keeps the physical discomfort we feel in check and tells our body that everything is okay even during uncomfortable physiological arousal, which then signals to our brain that the situation isn't as bad as it seems.

Smiling in the midst of stress is a good example of practicing Opposite Action. "Facial coding" experiments by psychologist Paul Ekman confirmed that adopting a "Duchenne smile," which is a full smile that involves using the facial muscles around the eyes, produced changes in brain activity that accompanied a better mood. New studies also confirmed that "Smilers" – those who adopt a smile after completing a stressful task – had lowered heart rates than those who adopted neutral expressions. Although it may seem artificial to smile in the midst of stressful situation at first, your mood will become elevated and your stress levels will be lowered. Your brain won't know the difference (Dooley 2013).

Mindfulness Body Relaxation Techniques - You can use Body Scan Relaxation meditations to help you with this process - these meditations help you to be mindful of each body part and relieve tension throughout. These meditations involve tensing and then relaxing muscles, which is the process of exaggerating the tension in our face, stomach or other problem areas, and then letting that tension go. This reveals to us how much tension we're carrying around and allows us to feel more at ease with our own bodies which carry the burden of our emotional stress.

Mindful Breathing techniques are usually coupled with these and you can envision your breath as an agent, relieving the tension throughout your body. These relaxation processes are a productive way to rechannel your inactivity into productive stillness. I recommend researching different types of mindful breathing techniques and finding meditations that suit your needs. You can find some recommendations at the online tools list at the end of this chapter.

Exercise - I mentioned it before as part of your self-care regimen and I'll mention it again because it's that important. This has always been the go-to stress reliever package. We've heard time and time again that exercise releases endorphins, chemicals which interact with receptors in our brain that change our perception of pain, and leave us feeling happier and more content. As an added bonus, exercise keeps us healthy, active and alert. But besides running on the treadmill, Yoga and Pilates can be amazing forms of exercise that relieve tension and anxiety. Yoga and Pilates both focus on the integration of breath and body, so it is like a hybrid of meditation and an intense workout. By practicing either, you are more prepared to relax during times of physical tension while also releasing those helpful endorphins that relieve stress.

Sensory Awareness Practice - This type of meditation can come through a meditation podcast or as your own self- designed exercise. All you need are your senses and a willingness to observe everything around you. Whether you're in a beautiful setting or the dreary interior of an office space, noticing details like the feeling of your feet upon the ground, the smell of coffee, or a beautiful sunset can all enhance your attention to the present moment. If the present moment is taking place in a context that is aesthetically pleasing like a park or the beach, this technique is even more effective in enhancing your experience of the joys of everyday life.

Hobbies - Hobbies should always be in our self-care toolbox. What do you like to do outside of your professional life and relationships that enhances your own quality time with yourself? Writing in a journal, scrapbooking, photography, rock climbing, collecting beautiful objects - these are all great hobbies to engage in to remind ourselves that there is an "inner life" within each of us that deserves to be nourished and keep ourselves focused more intensely on present activities. Our ability to creatively interact with life, and our intelligence and discipline in doing so gives us some necessary "me" time which grants us the space for personal growth.

Mantras and Positive Affirmations– Think of a mantra as an "Opposite Action" in itself, because it is the very opposite of an obsessive thought or fear. Similar to the self-affirmations listed previously, mantras are also a great way to reconnect with the present moment. Mantras are phrases or words that we find calming to us during stressful times. Mantras can act upon the subconscious in powerful ways and help us to behave in our best interests. It's important to have a mantra that's customized to your needs and specific fears or triggers. A mantra like, "I am beautiful and cherished," for example, may be useful to someone who has fears about not being loved or not being appreciated and who suffers from constant triggers of past mistreatment in his or her environment.

Mantras rechannel the ruminating process and bring the awareness back to you, centering you within positivity, encouragement and acceptance. Mantras can be used daily during a specific time of day, or during a particular meditation exercise. It depends on what works for you and what you find most effective. Find a way to integrate your mantra into daily activities. For example, I like to use mantras while I go about my daily errands.

WHY MINDFULNESS WORKS: YOUR BRAIN ON MINDFULNESS

A crucial way mindfulness works as a vehicle for emotion regulation is through actual changes in the neural networks of the brain. Studies (Farb, Anderson and Segal 2012) on the neural benefits of mindfulness in the way we approach our emotions show the following:

The engagement of open, present-moment attention helps to reduce cognitive rumination, a pattern of self-critical elaboration which is linked to prefrontal cortex reactivity that is seen in depressed patients.

Conscious awareness of our emotions disrupt habitual dysphoric reactions and allows for healthier approaches such as self-compassion and acceptance, which enables us to practice better self-care. When we're more aware of our emotions and less reactive, we're less likely to be impulsive and engage in unhealthy coping mechanisms when confronted with pain.

Mindful emotional regulation increases emotional awareness by reducing midline prefrontal reactivity and more sustained limbic network activation. This decreased activation in cortical midline structures is often related to negative mood induction, self-referential judgments and negative self-beliefs, so mindfulness disrupts and suspends negative or self-critical appraisal associated with cortical midline activity.

The intentional cultivation of awareness towards emotional information eliminates subliminal priming effects on preferences, engages greater prefrontal cortical resources and evokes less of an amygdala response. The amygdala is the part of the brain that processes emotions and the prefrontal cortex is involved with decision-making and impulse control. Mindfulness reduces automatic affective processing because it leads to non-reactivity in the amygdala in the face of negative emotional events. **So mindfulness helps us to become less impulsive and more able to cope with our emotions effectively.**

Mindfulness promotes activation of the right-lateralized network in the insula and secondary somatosensory cortices, which support more of a detached, somatic and objective awareness of the "self." Mindfulness also helps us to develop a stronger prefrontal attention network through focused attention to sensations from the body. **This somatic and objective awareness of the self helps us to observe and describe the present moment (in the form of bodily sensations) rather than getting "stuck" on our emotions.**

There is also a great deal of evidence to support the positive changes that mindfulness-focused meditation causes in the brain. Studies (Brown and Ryan, 2003; Creswell, Eisenberger, and Lieberman, 2007; Gladding, 2013; Pederson 2013; Malinowski, 2013) show the following:

Meditation literally changes crucial neural connections in the brain that enable us to cope better with sensations of anxiety and stress, allowing us to respond these sensations more productively. As a result, we are more prepared to cope with challenging situations.

Meditation literally changes gene expression which counter the "fight or flight" stress response, shapes the brain's neural networks to benefit the way our brain responds to stress and allocates attentional resources more efficiently.

In expert meditators, mindfulness meditation creates an altered relationship with pain so that there is a decoupling of affective appraisal and the primary sensation of pain.

Meditation introduces a pattern of brain connectivity that recruits auditory, thalamic, limbic and insular cortices. This refined integration promotes conscious awareness and prevents distraction, allowing for the full engagement required of mindfulness.

Meditation increases grey matter volume in interoceptive and sensory regions such as the insula, somatosensory cortex and parietal regions, while decreasing grey matter volume related to stress. It increases activity among the limbic system, thalamus, anterior cingulate cortex, and lateral prefrontal cortex when prompted to mindfully respond to emotionally provocative stimuli.

This reduces the tendency of an individual to act impulsively in response to emotionally arousing stimuli.

Meditation restores autonomy to the central executive system and frees it from habitual responses – enabling us to see the world in ways that are free from habitual and likely maladaptive ways of thinking.

Like mindful attention, the non-judgmental attention of meditation allows for emergent feelings of self-compassion which can help curb an individual's negative response to unpleasant events and feed into new, more helpful and balanced conceptual interpretations of situations.

Remember, the present moment is really all we have for certain. We should always try to enjoy the beauty and happiness of it, or at the very least, create a sense of relaxation and contentment that enhances our overall joy in life. The reason mindfulness works – both as a practice and as a way of life- is that it literally creates changes in the brain so that we're less emotionally impulsive, more compassionate towards ourselves, and more able to cope with stressful situations.

HELPFUL ONLINE RESOURCES AND TOOLS

Guidelines for meditation can be found here:
http://www.meditationoasis.com/how-to-meditate/general-guidelines/

Learn more about mindfulness here:
http://dbtselfhelp.com/html/mindfulness.html

Learn more about opposite action here:
http://dbtselfhelp.com/html/opposite_action.html

Look at the Pleasurable Activities List here:
http://www.dbtselfhelp.com/html/er_handout_8.html

Learn more about mantras here:
http://www.chopra.com/community/online-library/terms/mantra

Learn more about the anxiety cycle here:
http://www.morninglightcounseling.org/images/stories/p df/CBT_Handouts/Decatastrophizing.pdf

Learn more about radical acceptance here:
http://www.dbtselfhelp.com/html/radical_acceptance_
pa rt_1.html

5   CURBING NEGATIVE SELF-TALK

Negative thinking manifests in self-fulfilling prophecies. Don't believe me? All you have to do is research studies like Jacobson and Rosenthal's Pygmalion Effect or look up studies that demonstrate the power of stereotype threat on task performance to acknowledge this is true (Jacobson and Rosenthal, 1968). For example, experiments on stereotype threat reveal that a stereotype such as "Girls are worse in math" can hinder performance on mathematics tests by dedicating more of our working memory to the threat of the stereotype being true rather than to the task at hand (Spencer, Steele and Quinn, 1999). These studies reveal the consequences of labeling, stereotypes and negative beliefs that ultimately undermine performance and encourage maladaptive behavior. Trauma therapist calls the habitual negative thinking resulting from trauma or abuse "the inner critic." Someone who has a rather aggressive inner critic shames herself and believes she is incapable of achieving. It feeds into a negative feedback loop – a vicious cycle where the more she speaks negatively to herself, the more she underachieves because the less she expects to succeed. Essentially, the greater people are expected to perform, the greater they actually do. What do you think happens when people believe they can't do something? You got it – they trick themselves into thinking they can't and the belief becomes so ingrained in them that they barely try. They essentially set themselves up for failure.

I believe this definitely applies to what we expect of ourselves and how we speak to ourselves on a daily basis. Self-labeling with beliefs like "I am not good enough," or "I don't deserve love," are powerful impediments to your success and self-care. It creates subconscious programs of defeat – and according to Dr. Bruce Lipton, author of *The Biology of Belief*, the majority of our behavior is actually driven by these subconscious beliefs that we may not even be aware of. Add negative thinking onto those existing core beliefs and you get a recipe for manifestation disaster! What you think, you may ultimately become. Even if you are partially resistant to your self-fulfilling prophecy, there will always be a part of you that does not believe in yourself fully. That partial outcome means we're not living up to our highest expectations. How do we untangle ourselves from our own self-criticism and stop standing in our own way? Here are some ways:

Rewrite the negativity of the past and make it a learning experience. Approach each new day with a clean slate. Forgive yourself from your own mistakes. Think of each new day as a new beginning and free yourself from the burdens and baggage that hold you back. Make the choice to believe in happiness.

How? A useful technique would be recalling what happened yesterday and remembering the positive and turning the negative into a constructive learning experience. Do a step-by-step follow-up to whatever happened yesterday and spend fifteen minutes remembering the events, people, places and/or comments that made you smile. When you remember something negative, take a deep, cleansing breath and try to place a meaning on the negative event that occurred. For example, were you late to an important meeting? Did you have a fight with your brother? Was there an accident you witnessed on the way home?

When something negative comes up, try to figure out if any productive results occurred as a result. Did the fight you had with your brother lead to a better understanding of each other's needs? Did your tardiness lead you to be more mindful of all the work assignments that needed to get done, and motivate you to be more on time in the future? Did the horrible accident remind you of how precious and short life is?

Every event can be learned from and every experience can have a productive result, so long as you channel its meaning into positive change. As for reliving the positive events, it's always a good idea to dig out the nuances of each day. Chances are, even a seemingly terrible day will have some good in it, and if you take the time to relish that, you open yourself up to a lesson in how you can increase those types of positive events in the future. You can also maximize the positive by planning more of the positive events that occurred in the future (if you noticed that you had a good time laughing at a comedy skit, for example, you might want to schedule that into your daily routine.)

Be grateful for the present. Studies show that grateful people are happier people (Watkins, Woodward, Stone and Kolts, 2003). If you write in a gratitude journal or take a few minutes each day to remind yourself of all the blessings in your life, you will cultivate a long-term sense of well-being and happiness. Cultivating a lifelong habit of gratitude will do wonders for your happiness. It's been proven time and time again that grateful people cherish even the smallest joys of life and also have fewer prerequisites that need to be filled before they experience joy. Some people enjoy taking the time to be grateful during meditation; some write; some pray. What's important is to choose whatever technique works for you and is in sync with your beliefs and values. Even if it's just taking yourself to a quiet place in nature and relaxing in the silence, noting every little good thing that happened that day, you should make time for it because it's an effective way to give you an extra dose of happiness.

How? If you're having trouble feeling grateful, I suggest taking the time to remember the basic things you take for granted all the time and creating a list you can refer to. How about your sight? Your ability to hear? To taste? Your legs, your arms, the ability to dance, to run, to walk, to play, to work? Not everyone has these abilities and you should feel blessed for every advantage you have in your life.

Perhaps you're a perfectionist and compare yourself to others; remind yourself that just as there are people who appear more successful, there are also people who are struggling and would love to be in your exact position for the same blessings you take for granted every day. Think of every obstacle and struggle as an opportunity for growth. Remember: every challenge presents an opportunity to prove yourself and push yourself beyond your self-imposed limits.

Reexamine your negative attitudes. There's no doubt that there are harsh traumas and negative events that you may face in your life. There's also no doubt that these are painful and difficult to overcome. However, your attitude towards those events also determines your ability to surpass them and become a more successful person as a result. It's okay to feel sad, anxious, depressed, hurt, scared, and angry. You should always validate your own feelings, even if nobody else around you understands them. It's also okay to heal and to let go after validating and processing these feelings. There isn't a reason to hang onto them; if you feel yourself letting go of some negative emotions, don't try to bring yourself back to the same stage again. Understand that while you went through this horrific pain, you can now bring yourself to a higher mental and spiritual state. Harness your rage and sadness into constructive outlets like writing, jogging, or serving the community. Make your pain productive to yourself and others.

How? So many situations are outside of our control, but it's possible that you may hold the power to at least alleviate some of the pain or anxiety that come with some of these situations. For example, can you choose to meditate more on more difficult days? Can you make an effort to smile and enjoy your day despite someone unloading their negative baggage on you? Can you choose to take time out for yourself, a mini-vacation to relieve yourself of work-related stress? Can you bring yourself to a mindset of gratitude even in the most trying of times?

Can you surround yourself with some pleasurable distractions even while you wait out the strife? Can you use your painful experiences and traumas to speak out and shed light on social justice issues like domestic violence or bullying? Can you use your intuitive, compassionate nature to help others in need or in similar situations as yourself? Can you find something to laugh about? Can you use your anger to propel your voice forward and regain your inner power and strength?

The truth is you can do all of these even though it may be difficult. You have to constantly keep practicing this ability across diverse situations and contexts. Allow yourself room for mistakes. Acknowledge when you haven't done your best. Then try, try, and try again.

Reinforce your boundaries. We've talked a lot about setting boundaries with others and ending negative relationships that drain you more than sustain you. But what about setting boundaries with yourself? Limit the negative self-talk. Banish the browbeating inner voice. When you find yourself thinking badly of yourself or your abilities or the stage you're in at your life, make a positive space where you can celebrate all the positive things about you.

How? This is where therapies like Cognitive Behavioral Therapy or hypnotherapy can be helpful. Find a therapist who is validating and willing to work with you on self-sabotaging beliefs that may be holding you back in the areas of relationships, success, love, and self-love. As mentioned before, you may need to make a list of compliments others have given you before moving on to making a list of things you love and like and appreciate about yourself as part of a reverse discourse about yourself. Or a list of accomplishments and goals. Whatever list you start with, begin it today. Keep it on your bulletin board or in your favorite book, somewhere accessible.

Have a daily set of positive affirmations that calm you, like, "I am beautiful inside and out," or "I am talented" in times of self-doubt. Try a simple exercise such as jotting down the every day thoughts of your "inner critic" in a "Feelings and Thoughts" diary to track your every day ruminations, if you do suffer from obsessive and degrading thoughts. Have a 'redirecting' thought or pattern-interrupting behavior that disrupts the pattern of negative thinking.

For example, every time you find yourself swept up in a black hole of self-judgment, go to the mirror and say a few loving, gentle things to yourself. This is what self-help author Louise Hay calls 'mirror work' and it can really help to reconnect you with your own sense of self-compassion – especially when you're forced to look into your own eyes and recognize your own humanity. You are only human, just like anyone else. You have flaws, scars and shortcomings – but you also have strength, drive, perseverance and beauty. Find little things you like about yourself – from the color of your hair to your toothy smile. Celebrate your inner qualities as well. Create an entire dialogue, if you have to! Tell yourself in the mirror, "I see you. You're more gorgeous and smart than you give yourself credit for. You are so worthy, darling. So stop beating yourself up and start building yourself up." Invite a gentler narrative. There's something about seeing yourself while talking to yourself that can bring even the worst inner critic to its knees.

If you find mirror work difficult, go for a jog until the rush of endorphins give you something nicer to think about – like how good your body feels when you treat it right! Call a friend who always knows how to reassure you and reaffirms how precious you are – sometimes social support can facilitate our own approval – even though we don't want to become dependent upon it. Be your own best friend and treat yourself as such by saying, "Oh no, I am not letting you talk to me like that!" Set yourself reminders on your phone that say, "Remember three nice things about yourself today" on a daily basis.

Seriously - find creative ways to break the pattern, over and over again, until you've significantly reduced your pattern of negative self-talk and replaced it with healthier, more compassionate ways of speaking to yourself and seeing yourself.

Remind yourself of your dreams and of all the positive things that have happened thus far. In the midst of all the struggle, negative self-criticism will only beat you down further and serve as an impediment to your victory. You deserve to be victorious. Once you believe it, you will accomplish it, and you will enable your life to become as positive as the thoughts you permit in your mind.

HELPFUL RESOURCES AND TOOLS:

Cognitive distortions handout:
http://www.morninglightcounseling.org/images/stories
/pdf/C
BT_Handouts/10_Forms_of_Twisted_Thinking.pdf

Cultivating positive awareness:
http://www.morninglightcounseling.org/images/stories
/pdf/C BT_Handouts/Gratitude_Journal.pdf

Positive Thinking Handout:
http://www.mindtools.com/pages/article/newTCS_06.
htm

Creating a Gratitude Journal:
http://greatergood.berkeley.edu/article/item/tips_for_k
eeping_a_ gratitude_journal/

Positive Affirmations Hypnosis by Joseph Clough
http://josephclough.com/blog/positive-affirmations-
hypnosis- free-mp3-download/

6 RECOVERY FROM EMOTIONAL

TRAUMA

Emotional abuse consists of a series of unhealthy behavior patterns in which a partner intentionally inflicts harm on another by undermining his or her self-worth and confidence, manipulates the other person into believing he/she is crazy (also known as "gaslighting") so that the person may doubt his/her sanity and subjects the victim to continuous verbal and psychological abuse. Often, emotional abuse is inflicted by those who have maladaptive interpersonal styles and traumas of their own.

These abusers may have come from abusive households themselves and may be modeling behaviors they've learned from childhood. Other times, emotional abuse is inflicted by malignant narcissists who lack empathy or sociopaths who lack conscience. A lack of conscience is eerily more common than we would like to think. According to Harvard psychologist Martha Stout (2005), 1 in 25 of people in the United States can be classified as a sociopath. Whatever the reasons behind the abuse may be, the impact of the abuse is undoubtedly devastating and a deficient self-care regimen can leave us even more vulnerable to predators, exploiters and abusers.

In order to engage in effective self-care, it is absolutely necessary to end relationships that are or have the potential to become emotionally abusive or unhealthy. What makes ending these relationships so difficult is that the abuser usually makes the victim so dependent and doubtful that he or she feels unable to leave.

Abusers seek out targets that usually already have issues with self-esteem, which is a key reason why it is important to learn more about your own boundaries, values and relationship patterns. It is essential to develop a high sense of self-love and independence before getting into a long-term relationship with anyone. We cannot "fix" or "save" anybody but ourselves. Essentially, if it seems you're dating someone with the mindset of a child rather than an adult, it's time to stop emotionally babysitting and get a full-time job taking care of YOU.

The RED FLAGS to watch out for when beginning a new relationship include:

Signs of excessive jealousy/insecurity, especially comments regarding what you can or cannot do (e.g. "you cannot go out dancing with friends," "you cannot hang out with this person") or interrogations about your life, your friends, your activities, your job or any facet of life that does not include the partner.

Unnecessarily critical comments about one's competence, job, appearance, friends, family, etc. Comments that are not meant to be constructive but are rather said with spite or condescension. These comments can also be masked as "brutal honesty" or "helpful" remarks which are actually part of an elaborate power play to ridicule or demean you.

Name-calling, profanity, excessive sarcasm and/or ridiculing your thoughts, feelings or decisions. For example, calling you "oversensitive" in response to harsh teasing or jokes, calling you "crazy" if you express your emotions, cursing at you if the abuser dislikes something you tell them.

Chronic cheating (emotionally or physically) and lying. Cheating can be emotional as well as physical. Partners can flirt, confide in or promise other women things without even so much as a kiss or the breaking of a physical boundary. Remember anything your partner does that makes you feel uncomfortable and be sure to assess it to see whether your discomfort is coming from the trespassing of an emotional boundary or from your own jealousy issues.

Know the difference. Talking to and hanging out with a female friend is OK, but flirting with and making suggestive comments to such a friend is not (unless you have more flexible boundaries that apply to both of you, which, in that case, stick with your own values and assess accordingly). Be alert to the fact that emotional abusers WILL call you jealous and insecure if you bring up things that make you feel uncomfortable. Physical cheating is almost easier to call out because there are less gray areas to negotiate (although an abuser will probably deny, lie or minimize the extent to which they cheat).

Denying you your right to feel and perceive things the way you do or making you feel emotionally or physically unsafe to do so. Comments about how "crazy" or "sensitive" you are whenever you assert yourself or say something the person doesn't agree with. As mentioned earlier, this is a technique known as gaslighting. This enables the abuser to cast doubt on your perceptions of things, so that you devalue your feelings of discomfort and forego your intuition. In fact, the abuser invalidates you so that you in turn begin to invalidate yourself. The abuser will probably claim you are the only person who's ever had a problem with his behavior, or deny saying something you remember him saying.

Physical aggression. This can be blatantly obvious or subtle. Whether a partner finds ways to "sneak in" aggression by grabbing your arm too harshly during an argument or pushes you away with force, it is still abusive.

Controlling and hurtful comments about what you should wear, what looks good on you, your weight, your figure, your eating habits etc. Abusers with deep-seated issues regarding their own appearance or self-esteem will often project these insecurities onto their victims so that they feel better about themselves. Don't think that just because you're dating someone who's technically less attractive than you that they won't find ways to demean you or abuse you. In fact, that just gives abusers more motivation to bring you down, to convince you that you are nothing without them and unworthy of someone better.

Comments that compare you to other people in terms of appearance, competence, success, etc. These are degrading comments that serve no other purpose but to make the abuser feel powerful and in control. Even innocent remarks like "She doesn't do this" can become toxic if they are said repeatedly with the intent of putting you down and comparing you to others.

Triangulation which is basically bringing another person into the relationship either by talking about them or physically bringing them into the picture. This is a favorite technique of sociopaths and narcissists in particular to enhance the appearance of their desirability (see "Narcissistic Abuse" section below for more information). It can even happen with complete strangers that do not know your narcissistic abuser – so long as he is able to charm them into talking to him in front of you (waiters and waitresses are a great example) you will find yourself looking at the same manipulatively charming man who once wooed you – now wooing a complete stranger with no seeming benefit except to rile you up and get you to compete.

Bringing up other exes, lovers, former lovers, crushes by openly talking to them through social media, physically bringing them into the space of your interactions or by mentioning them excessively in your conversations, are all part of narcissists' elaborate schemes to stroke their own egos and get you to compete for their affections. It titillates them that you do this (and if they fit into the narcissistic or sociopathic category, believe me, they know exactly what they are doing) because it validates their excessive need for attention.

It doesn't matter who is in the triangle with you – in fact, abusers bring in anyone and everyone, regardless of how they may look or act. So beware of this in the early stages of a relationship (if it happens excessively, that's a clue that something is a bit off and requires further investigation).

Also beware of **white lies or big lies** early on in the relationship that the abuser claims are "misunderstandings" or things he has "misspoken" about. These are definite red flags that dishonesty is part of your partner's relationship pattern.

Cycling of "hot" and "cold" behavior. Emotional abusers can be very sweet, manipulative and subject you to a hot "honeymoon" phase where there's a sense of abuse amnesia, and you feel convinced that his abuse isn't as bad as you thought it was. In reality, you minimize and deny the existence of the abuse because you feel he "didn't mean to" and he's "acting so much better now."

Of course, abusers will soon go back to their abusive behavior and continue the vicious cycle of abuse, retreating and coming back with full force – apologies, sweet-talking, gifts, surprises...don't be fooled. This is all part of their mask and it may remind you of better times in the early stages of a relationship. You may be tempted into thinking this means the abuser has changed and is genuinely looking to correct their ways. The truth is, they are simply reeling you in with the fantasy they first presented to you. It is all just a mask to hide their true selves.

Excessive stonewalling and emotional withdrawal. In a healthy relationship, there will always be times when the other person might want to cool down before talking about important issues. So long as this is communicated in a respectful manner and is done with consideration to one's feelings, this is not a problem. However, in an abusive relationship, you will find yourself being abruptly stonewalled with the same catchphrases over and over again ("Shut up!" "We're done!" "I am done!" "You're crazy!"). Conversations where you bring up emotions and problems in the relationship will automatically be shut down. You will be forced to deal with the silent treatment as you struggle to apologize and understand what you did wrong. This silent treatment can last for a short period or longer periods, but the length of time isn't as important as the fact that it's a way to control and regulate your normal emotional response to abuse, a way to demonstrate that your emotions and thoughts do not matter. If this happens more than twice, you can be sure it's part of a larger maladaptive behavioral pattern that will not end.

As you become conditioned to not receiving the satisfaction of healthy communication or resolution regarding issues in the relationship, you start to silence yourself more and tend to swallow both your words and rage. Abusers can also physically or emotionally distance themselves from you in other ways, so be wary of a lack of affection in public or shutting down especially if you feel you have done nothing wrong or if this is not the norm during your "honeymoon" stage.

Doubt, fear and anxiety over his or her feedback. You find yourself spending a great deal of time ruminating over spiteful comments and insults, wondering if they are in fact correct, wondering what you did to provoke them, blaming yourself while thinking the person is right or hating the person and absolving yourself of responsibility (emotional polarization also known as "splitting"), slowly coming to internalize the abuse.

You develop a sense of learned helplessness, which is a feeling of being unable to control your external environment after many failed attempts to avoid aversive stimuli. Seligman's (1972) famous study of dogs who received electric shocks showed that these dogs stopped attempting to escape even when escaping the shocks became easy. In the framework of emotional abuse, these early attempts include trying to argue with the abuser, trying to get the abuser to see your point of view, and essentially educating a grown person on what basic respect and decency implies, with no result other than stonewalling or another "honeymoon" phase before the abuse starts again.

This feeling of learned helplessness can become generalized and extended to all other facets of your life outside of the relationship, depleting your emotional reserves and self-esteem. As you internalize the abuse, you find yourself feeling worthless, hopeless, and unable to leave the relationship. The person has stripped you of your confidence and has ultimately immobilized you. You don't wish to stay, but you also feel a lack of agency due to your diminished sense of importance.

NARCISSISTIC ABUSE

Please note: Cheating and other invalidating forms of emotional abuse are especially difficult things to call out if you are involved with a narcissistic abuser who will deny or lie about the cheating without any remorse and who will employ specific covert manipulation tactics that deny the abuse altogether.

Narcissistic abusers are masters of making you feel like the insecure one even if they are the one continually breaking boundaries behind your back. These are abusers who meet the criteria for Narcissistic Personality Disorder. They are characterized by their excessive need for attention and admiration, a construction of a "false" superficial self that interacts charmingly with others, and a habit of exploiting others without remorse. If you want to emotionally exhaust yourself with no positive return on your investment, date a narcissist. Those with Antisocial Personality Disorder take it one step further; they not only lack empathy but they lack a conscience and routinely violate the personal boundaries of others in even more criminal ways.

WHAT IS A NARCISSIST?

In popular culture, the term "narcissistic" is thrown about quite loosely, usually referring to vanity and self-absorption. This reduces narcissism to a common quality that everyone possesses and downplays the symptoms demonstrated by people with the actual disorder. While narcissism does exist on a spectrum, narcissism as a full-fledged personality disorder is quite different.

People who meet the criteria for Narcissistic Personality Disorder or those who have traits of Antisocial Personality Disorder can operate in extremely manipulative ways within the context of intimate relationships due to their deceitfulness, lack of empathy and their tendency to be interpersonally exploitative. Although I will be focusing on narcissistic abusers in this post, due to the overlap of symptoms in these two disorders, this list can potentially apply to interactions with those who have ASPD to an extent.

You will find evidence for all these tactics in popular books about sociopaths and narcissists, as well as anecdotal evidence from thousands of abuse survivors who share similar stories. If you'd like to learn more about narcissism or psychopathy outside of this book, I'd suggest reading Psychopath Free by Peace, Malignant Self-Love by Sam Vaknin, The Sociopath Next Door by Martha Stout, It's All About Him by Lisa E. Scott and Narcissistic Lovers: How to Cope, Recover, and Move On by Cynthia Zayn and M.S. Kevin Dibble.

It's important in any kind of relationship that we learn to identify the red flags when interacting with people who display malignant narcissism and/or antisocial traits, so we can better protect ourselves from exploitation and abuse, set boundaries, and make informed decisions about who we keep in our lives. Understanding the nature of these toxic interactions and how they affect us has an enormous impact on our ability to engage in self-care.

FIVE COVERT MANIPULATION TACTICS OF THE NARCISSTIC ABUSER

Watch out for the following covert manipulation tactics when you're dating someone or in a relationship.

1. The Idealization-Devaluation-Discard Phase

Narcissists and those with antisocial traits tend to subject romantic partners through three phases within a relationship. The idealization phase (which often happens most strongly during the early stages of dating or a relationship) consists of putting you on a pedestal, making you the center of his/her world, being in contact with you frequently, and showering you with flattery and praise. You are convinced that the narcissist can't live without you and that you've met your soulmate. Be wary of: constant texting, shallow flattery and wanting to be around you at all times. This is a technique known as "love-bombing" and it is how most victims get sucked in: they are tired of the "games" people play with each other in communication and are flattered by the constant attention they get from the narcissist. You may be fooled into thinking that this means a narcissist is truly interested in you, when in fact, he or she is interested in making you dependent on their constant praise and attention.

The devaluation phase is subsequent to this idealization phase, and this is when you're left wondering why you were so abruptly thrust off the pedestal. The narcissist will suddenly start to blow hot and cold, criticizing you, covertly and overtly putting you down, comparing you to others, emotionally withdrawing from you and giving you the silent treatment when you've failed to meet their "standards." Since the "hot" aspect of this phase relies on intermittent reinforcement in which the narcissist gives you inconsistent spurts of the idealization phase throughout, you become convinced that perhaps you are at fault and you can "control" the narcissist's reactions.

Even though the narcissist can be quite possessive and jealous over you, since he or she views you as an object and a source of narcissistic supply, the narcissist is prone to projecting this same behavior onto you. The narcissist makes you seem like the needy one as you react to his or her withdrawal and withholding patterns even though the expectations of frequent contact were established early on in the relationship by the narcissist himself.

You are mislead into thinking that if you just learn not to be so "needy," "clingy," or "jealous," the narcissist will reward you with the loving behavior he or she demonstrated in the beginning. The narcissist may use these and other similar words to gaslight victims when they react normally to being provoked. It's a way to maintain control over your legitimate emotional reactions to their stonewalling, emotional withdrawal and inconsistency.

Unfortunately, it is during the devaluation phase that a narcissist's true self shows itself. You have to understand that the man or woman in the beginning of the relationship never truly existed. The true colors are only now beginning to show, so it will be a struggle as you attempt to reconcile the image that the narcissist presented to you with his or her current behavior.

During the discard phase, the narcissist abandons his or her victim in the most horrific, demeaning way possible to convince the victim that he or she is worthless. This could range from: leaving the victim for another lover, humiliating the victim in public, being physically aggressive and a whole range of other demeaning behaviors to communicate to the victim that he or she is no longer important.

2. Gaslighting.

Most abusive relationships contain a certain amount of gaslighting, a technique narcissists use to convince you that your perception of the abuse is inaccurate. During the devaluation and discard phases, the narcissist will often remark upon your emotional instability, your "issues," and displace blame of his/her abuse as your fault. Frequent use of phrases such as "You provoked me," "You're too sensitive," "I never said that," or "You're taking things too seriously" after the narcissists' abusive outbursts are common and are used to gaslight you into thinking that the abuse is indeed your fault or that it never even took place.

Narcissists are masters of making you doubt yourself and the abuse. This is why victims so often suffer from ruminations after the ending of a relationship with a narcissist, because the emotional invalidation they received from the narcissist made them feel powerless in their agency and perceptions. This self-doubt enables them to stay within abusive relationships even when it's clear that the relationship is a toxic one, because they are led to mistrust their own instincts and interpretations of events.

3. Smear campaigns.

Narcissists keep harems because they love to have their egos stroked and they need constant validation from the outside world to feed their need for excessive admiration and confirm their grandiose sense of self-importance. They are clever chameleons who are also people-pleasers, morphing into whatever personality suits them in situations with different types of people. It is no surprise, then, that the narcissist is likely to run a smear campaign against you not too long after the discard phase, in order to paint you as the unstable one, and that this is usually successful with the narcissist's support network which also tends to consist of other narcissists, people-pleasers, empaths, as well as people who are easily charmed.

This smear campaign accomplishes three things: 1) it depicts you as the abuser or unstable person and deflects your accusations of abuse, 2) it provokes you, thus proving your instability to others when trying to argue his or her depiction of you, and 3) serves as a hoovering technique in which the narcissist seeks to pull you back into the trauma of the relationship as you struggle to reconcile the rumors about you with who you actually are by speaking out against the accusations. The only way to not get pulled into this tactic is by going full No Contact with both the narcissist and his or her harem.

4. Triangulation.

Healthy relationships thrive on security; unhealthy ones are filled with provocation, uncertainty and infidelity. Narcissists like to manufacture love triangles and bring in the opinions of others to validate their point of view. They do this to an excessive extent in order to play puppeteer to your emotions. In the book Psychopath Free by Peace, the method of triangulation is discussed as a popular way the narcissist maintains control over your emotions. Triangulation consists of bringing the presence of another person into the dynamic of the relationship, whether it be an ex-lover, a current mistress, a relative, or a complete stranger.

This triangulation can take place over social media, in person, or even through the narcissist's own verbal accounts of the other woman or man. The narcissist relies on jealousy as a powerful emotion that can cause you to compete for his or her affections, so provocative statements like "I wish you'd be more like her," or "He wants me back into his life, I don't know what to do" are designed to trigger the abuse victim into competing and feeling insecure about his or her position in the narcissist's life.

Unlike healthy relationships where jealousy is communicated and dealt with in a productive manner, the narcissist will belittle your feelings and continue inappropriate flirtations and affairs without a second thought. Triangulation is the way the narcissist maintains control and keeps you in check - you're so busy competing for his or her attention that you're less likely to be focusing on the red flags within the relationship or looking for ways to get out of the relationship.

5. The false self and the true self.
The narcissist hides behind the armor of a "false self," a construct of qualities and traits that he or she usually

presents to the outside world. Due to this armor, you are unlikely to comprehend the full extent of a narcissist's inhumanity and lack of empathy until you are in the discard phase. This can make it difficult to pinpoint who the narcissistic abuser truly is - the sweet, charming and seemingly remorseful person that appears shortly after the abuse, or the abusive partner who ridicules, invalidates and belittles you on a daily basis?

You suffer a great deal of cognitive dissonance trying to reconcile the illusion the narcissist first presented to you with the tormenting behaviors he or she subjects you to. In order to cope with this cognitive dissonance, you might blame yourself for his or her abusive behavior and attempt to "improve" yourself when you have done nothing wrong, just to uphold your belief in the narcissist's false self during the devaluation phase.

During the discard phase, the narcissist reveals the true self - the ugly, abusive and abrasive monster rears its head and you get a glimpse of the evil that was lurking within all along. You bear witness to his or her cold, callous indifference as you are discarded. You might think this is only a momentary lapse into evil, but actually, it is as close you will ever get to seeing the narcissist's true self.

The manipulative, conniving charm that existed in the beginning is no more - instead, it is replaced by the genuine contempt that the narcissist felt for you all along. See, narcissists don't truly feel empathy or love for others - so during the discard phase, they feel absolutely nothing for you except the excitement of having exhausted another source of supply. You were just another source of supply, so do not fool yourself into thinking that the magical connection that existed in the beginning was in any way real. It was an illusion, much like the identity of the narcissist was an illusion.

It is time to pick up the pieces, go No Contact, heal, and move forward. You were not only a victim of narcissistic abuse, but a survivor. Owning this dual status as both victim and survivor permits you to own your agency after the abuse and to live the life you were meant to lead - one filled with self-care, self-love, respect, and compassion.

YOU REALIZED YOU WERE OR ARE A VICTIM OF ABUSE – SO WHAT DO YOU DO NOW?

Once you notice that the person you're dating or in a relationship with has these abusive tendencies, there are key things you MUST know:

It is absolutely in no way your fault. The way an abuser treats you and how he talks to you is about HIM and not you. Everyone has flaws and everyone has problems in relationships. However, these flaws and relationship problems should not ever give someone permission to degrade, abuse or invalidate you constantly. Do not ever bear the burden of blame for someone else's issues and abuse. Remember that this abuser will also (and probably has) abused others in his lifetime, even though he or she will probably claim that "you are the only one who has ever had this problem with me."

Do not ever fear that this person will "move on" and be happy and treat someone else more kindly. Remember that the abuser's treatment of you is enough to tell you exactly who this person is. Even if an abuser moves on and appears to be treating someone else better than he or she treated you, remember that this is only mirroring the happier, earlier stages of your own relationship with the abuser – the "honeymoon stage." It's also worth mentioning that other people may put up with more of the abuse than you do, acting as better doormats and having less boundaries. This may be the reason why THEIR relationship lasts as opposed to the relationship you had with the abuser, because you are not willing to put up with boundary-breaking and abuse.

If you're still not convinced that an abuser wouldn't treat their second or previous victims better than they treated you, let me tell you a story. A girl once approached me in the train station. She recognized me from social media and claimed we both had the same ex-boyfriend from the past. I was shocked to hear some of the stories she told me about the verbal and psychological abuse she suffered – at the hands of the same person I had dated years ago. I had always thought I was somehow "alone" in my abuse. Approaching me and sharing her story with me was not only tremendously brave, it gave me the confirmation of something I knew logically but resisted emotionally: you are not the first one, and unfortunately, you will not be the last one that suffers at the hands of an abuser.

Abusers have a way of isolating you in their gaslighting so that you feel responsible, telling you that "no one else has ever had this problem with me," and that "you're the only one who reacts this way." Don't be fooled! People may act differently with others, this is true. Narcissists especially are natural chameleons who put on masks to please different types of people. However, certain communication and interpersonal habits are difficult to get rid of and will eventually be exposed throughout the course of a close, intimate relationship. Getting closer to an abuser enables that abuser to vacillate between his "false self" and his true one, never quite giving you the full idealization he or she gave you in the early stages of a relationship.

Narcissistic abusers, for example, will idealize their targets, flattering them and making them the center of their world, before devaluing them and eventually, discarding them in horrific, heartless ways. Slowly but surely, the abuser can unravel this true self slowly until the break-up and this true self can manifest itself in the red flags mentioned previously. You just have to be willing to pay attention.

REMEMBER:

There are many people who do not live this way; you may have been conditioned to this pattern from an early age. Victims in emotionally abusive relationships can sometimes come from backgrounds of past abuse. They have often either experienced this emotional abuse in childhood or adolescence and have come to normalize and expect this line of behavior from past and present experience. It takes a while before the victim recognizes fully that this behavior is totally unacceptable (and by fully recognize, this means also leaving/ending the relationship). Be brave. Choose yourself over an abusive partner. Always and no matter what. No person can give you the unconditional love and care you desperately need to give to yourself.

It is important to remember that there are many people thriving in healthier, happier relationships that do not consist of any type of abuse. Which means a happy healthy relationship is not only possible, there is no reason for you not to leave this abusive, toxic one. This is why working with a counselor and doing research on your own relationship patterns is so vital and necessary in order to move forward into healthier and better relationships.

It's a fact that trauma can literally change and shape the way the brain works. In the most extreme cases, trauma can cause dissociative symptoms such as depersonalization or derealization where we feel detached from our experiences and from our own bodies. We can experience hypervigilance, numbing, intrusive thoughts and attempt to avoid any stimuli that reminds us of the trauma. The more we expose ourselves to trauma and prolong abusive relationships, the more likely our responses to future relationships will be maladaptive and unhealthy, and the more time will be needed to heal.

Your gut instincts/perceptions/emotions are valid. Always trust your intuition, especially in relationships. Abusive partners use a series of manipulative techniques to deny their victims' realities. Don't be fooled. Your emotions, instincts, thoughts and perceptions ARE valid. Going with your gut can save your life and your sanity. In an attempt to understand why this abuse is happening to us, we attempt to shift the blame to ourselves especially if the abuser has used the "gaslighting" technique on us.

It is important to remember that our gut instinct often tells us all we have to know. We don't have to continuously doubt our own perceptions, our thoughts, our emotions when we have the answer already within us. When you feel your worst within a relationship, it means *GET OUT*. This is one of those times you can indeed listen to your own body when it comes to interpreting the danger or threat of a situation. In this situation, the decision whether to submit to Fight or Flight should be simple: Flight.

Here are some tips for getting out of an emotionally abusive relationship:

Brainstorm a get-out plan according to the status of your relationship. Remember that this will depend specifically on your situation - your living situation, your sense of physical safety, and the severity of the abuse. Do what is comfortable and most safe for you and any other people involved, such as children or family members who are also at risk. If you need to detach slowly and then eventually cut all ties, do it. Or if you need to end ties with no communication whatsoever, do it. It all depends on your specific situation and the context. If you fight a lot face-to-face, it's probably not the best idea to do the break-up in person. If there is any threat of physical harm or imminent danger in breaking up with the person, DO NOT do so face-to-face. Always tell someone else about your whereabouts if you are involved in a relationship that has components of both emotional and physical abuse. Your safety comes first.

Last-Straw method. If it has come to the point where there has been a great deal of abuse and it is normalized, you probably aren't sure when will be the "turning point," the moment you decide to leave. A turning point is ultimately a change in the trajectory of the relationship. In many cases, you cannot just wait for it to happen. You have to create ripe conditions for the turning point to occur. So you must tell yourself, "The next time I feel disrespected, big or small, I leave."

Make that a commitment to yourself and make sure you tell a trusted friend or family member so they hold you to that commitment. If you live with the person and need to get out immediately, make sure you pack your essentials and be prepared to leave behind some things for the sake of your own sanity so you don't have to encounter this person again (if you must, have a third party pick up your things for you). The key is to physically leave even if you don't feel emotionally ready to do so. Make arrangements to stay with a friend or a family member and do not reveal where you are staying. If you must, give your phone to someone to avoid talking or picking up if the person calls.

Electronic communication has often been a cop-out for emotionally unavailable people, but don't feel guilty about simply texting, "I don't want to see you anymore" when things go too far or you cannot for whatever reason end the relationship in person. Your safety comes first.

Be ready to expect some serious manipulation, mind games, and/or insults if you attempt to "negotiate" any terms with an abuser. There is nothing to negotiate. You will not go back. You will not wait for them to change. You MUST make this commitment to yourself. Have at least one person (reliable and trustworthy) whom you can call should you have any urges to do otherwise.

Initiate No Contact as soon as the break-up is over. Keeping tabs on an emotionally and/or physically abusive ex-partner is like mourning the loss of trash after it has already been taken out. Remove and block your abuser and mutual friends or their family members from your phone and all social networking sites. You do not need constant reminders or triggers or any urges to contact them at any point after the break-up. With narcissistic abusers in particular, this is especially important because you can count on them to show off their new admirers and members of their harem. Resist the urge to stay "friends." Friends do not abuse each other in the way that your abuser did to you.

Rely on some outside networks to provide you information or resources you may need during this time. This can range from making arrangements with local shelters or reaching out to community organizations for domestic violence. You can look at the National Domestic Violence Hotline website here: http://www.thehotline.org/.

TIPS FOR RECOVERING FROM AN ABUSIVE RELATIONSHIP

Seek out professional help. Recovering from any type of abusive relationship takes work and you simply should not be doing it alone. The side effects of this form of trauma can be serious and long-lasting – you'll want a professional who is trauma-informed, validating and knowledgeable about domestic violence as well as the dynamics of more covert, insidious and emotional forms of abuse. Insight from a third party also helps give you perspective and hopefully reduce the urge to go back to the "safety blanket" of the abusive relationship. This is not to assume everyone can afford this type of help. Depending on your health insurance plan, whether or not you're in school (your school may provide mental health services for example) and where you live, the cost of professional help may be overwhelming. In any case, you should always be seeking out free or low-cost resources in your community and online, resources like an abuse survivors network, blogs about recovery from abuse, or events about the topic; these resources should not be undervalued, as every bit helps on your road to recovery.

Create a support network. If you do not have a strong support network either because your abuser was so controlling it was impossible to have one, or because you did not take the initiative to have one outside of the relationship, the important thing to realize is that it's never too late to create a support network. You can create one out of old friends and family members, but also remember that connecting with new people will reflect the new life you are creating. Attend support groups for abuse survivors, connect with people who have been there. Read relationship blogs, contribute to emotional abuse survivor forums and listen to mindfulness podcasts. Use Meetup as another way to connect with people who will be able to introduce you to activities that promote mental health (meditation and yoga meetups, for example).

Journaling. Writing is a terrific way to keep a track of your progress and write down whatever you're feeling or thinking. Use your journal as a safe space where you can be your authentic self and not be censored or silenced. This provides a clean, hopeful break from the unhealthy dynamics of your relationship, a place where you can reflect with freedom and validate your experiences without being berated or controlled. You can also keep track of your feelings and gut instincts about the new people you encounter, by noting the tactics your abuser used and recognizing similarities and/or differences. This will help you tune in more closely with your intuitive radar and keep you in check, lest you attract people into your life who are similar to your abuser (very possible, considering you're still in recovery mode).

Cultivate the positive image of yourself that accurately represents you, detached from the abuse you've experienced. Recovering from abuse means having to confront all the negative things your abuser claimed about you and all of the things you even believed about yourself. Use VISUAL and VERBAL aids mentioned earlier in the book to "silence" your abuser's claims and regain your voice. This means "talking back" to your abuser in a sense (this could be in your head, or speaking aloud, whichever method feels powerful to you) and creating that reverse discourse that challenges and undermines your abuser's words.

Some ideas might be: recording self-affirmations on a tape recorder and playing it back to yourself before sleeping or in the morning; creating a bulletin board filled with images of your accomplishments (e.g. graduation photos, awards) or motivational slogans; even creating a simple Pinterest board online that you can refer to every day, where you pin these slogans would do the trick. If you want to start simple, remember any and all the positive feedback people have given you and create a list from that. The point is to have a point of reference, something physical to look at and reference to help you come back to the mindful, powerful state that will ultimately help you overcome the abuse.

I also recommend reading self-help books and podcasts on a weekly basis because you will want to utilize every resource you have available. I personally love Joseph Clough's *Be Your Potential* self-hypnosis tracks which are available for almost every ailment and problem you can think of (health problems, relationship problems, problems focusing, among others). You can find the link to this at the end of the chapter. Even if you don't believe in hypnosis, approach the audio supplements as similar to meditation, something to soothe, motivate and heal you incrementally over time. You can cultivate your faith in this process over time, and even if it turns out to not be your thing, you'll at least know you tried different things to help your healing.

Remember: recovery is a challenging process, but it is a worthy one. I live by the philosophy that the day you mistreat and leave a good woman (or force her to leave you via abuse) is the day you gave her an opportunity to become a bad ass version of herself and find someone more worthy of her. Not only will you gain a greater sense of self, promote self-efficacy and bring back the power to you, you open yourself up to healthier relationships in the future without abuse.

GETTING OVER A BREAK-UP

There's no doubt about it: break-ups are emotionally, psychologically and physically devastating. They are messy, heartbreaking and terrible, even if you knew the person you were with wasn't the one for you. If you've experienced the pain of a break-up and survived it, congratulate yourself. If you've experienced it many times in multiple traumatic ways, YOU ARE A WARRIOR. You're a warrior, a victor, and a survivor of everything that has happened to you so far. If you've always told yourself things would never get better, it's time to start rewriting your own story. It does get better and it will. So be sure to end each chapter on a high note. Do not forget that. Of course, we all envy our friends who seemingly have been in long-term relationships for years, who've never had to go through such heartbreak. But remind yourself that those friends are often the ones who have also outgrown their relationships but are too afraid to leave the comfort and security of their relationships.

This isn't always the case and some people do get the lucky draw of their soulmate from an early age, but imagine trying to develop yourself while another person is always tagging along. Self-development is hard enough as it is without considering someone else's needs, wants and expectations. When constantly in a relationship, we have little time to fully explore our own interests, hobbies, dreams and goals without consulting someone else's opinions and feelings. So it's always good to have at least SOME time to yourself where you feel you can grow, independently, without the constant ups and downs of another person's whims. A break-up can be a tremendously rewarding journey because it's a signal that it's time to slow down, reevaluate our lives and understand ourselves better. It's a sign that we have to continue and improve our self- care regimen. Self-care is so important in times of crisis, and a break-up definitely qualifies.

THE FIRST FEW WEEKS AFTER THE BREAKUP

The first few weeks following the break-up are crucial because it is the period I call "crisis-mode." It's the feeling that your world is collapsing and you are barely keeping it together. You may also be very numb during this time and that is completely normal. Numbing is a normal response to trauma. It's the way your brain protects you from the impact of the shock and grief that will come later on. I have usually experienced break-ups similarly in that I always have a couple of days of complete shock where I am not feeling all my emotions. I know that my brain is protecting me, but I wishfully think and hope that this will be my emotional state forever. Unfortunately, we both know that is not the case. The numbness will pass, and the difficult emotions will come. Whether you deal with them in a healthy, productive way is a whole other question altogether.

You may suffer from not wanting to eat or wanting to overeat to bury your emotions. You may sleep too little or too much and feel unable to get up from bed in the morning. Maybe your symptoms aren't even that severe (if so, count yourself as one of the lucky ones!). Depending on the reasons for the breakup, how each party dealt with it, who broke up with who and how, how long and intense the relationship was, the extent to which there was abuse in the relationship, there will be multiple factors involved which will contribute to your current emotional state.

However, there are some universal ways you can cope with a break-up regardless of how long or abusive or beautiful or messy it was. Each relationship is different, so these coping mechanisms will have to be tailored to your particular needs for each ending of a relationship. Some break-ups will be harder than others, and you may even be surprised to discover that the length of a relationship doesn't necessarily dictate the amount of time you spend grieving or the amount of regrets you have.

This has to do with three factors: your level of commitment and investment in the relationship, how much time you spent with the other person, as well as your past experiences and emotional resilience which you've hopefully built up over time. Depending on WHEN the break-up happens, you will be more resilient and knowledgeable in certain break-ups than in others. For example, your first breakup will often be considerably harder to get over and let go of because you haven't yet developed coping methods for experiencing all of these complex emotions.

Here are some very important things to remember doing during these weeks:

Have a physical document that reminds you of why you're no longer in the relationship and the fact that you WILL get through this. You have to believe that you will survive and thrive, despite how much pain you feel right now. Writing down more about the toxic aspects of the relationship (or even writing an unsent letter to the ex) can be powerful and valuable in the first stages of the break-up. Having that physical document to remind you of why you are under no circumstances going back is necessary and vital in this stage of the process. Many books mention the "unsent letter" as a way to gain closure from an ex that never gave you any closure regarding why the break-up happened or the painful way it did happen.

The important thing is that while you do get all your thoughts and feelings out, you do not send this letter. Remember especially with abusers that any letter you send them will become a source of blackmail. Even if you manage to write the most mature, sophisticated letter known to mankind (which really wouldn't be helpful in honoring your authentic anger and despair because it would still be censored by certain boundaries and expectations), your ex can use this letter against you.

Also, you don't need to give them extra fuel for their ego after treating you so terribly - no need to show them that you're still thinking about them. If you do send the letter, you also risk the possibility that they will respond and say even more hurtful things to you out of pure spite. This will simply instigate more trauma and leave things even more messier than they already were.

Remain in minimum or no contact with your ex. You might contact your ex or get the urge to do so. Even though many break-up books advise going cold turkey and never contacting your ex again, I am a little more realistic. Sometimes getting burned twice or thrice will teach you not to go near the hot stove again. So if the urge to contact your ex feels overwhelming and unacceptable, creating an obsession that is even worse than the consequences of contacting your ex, you may end up giving into the urge.

That doesn't mean I condone contacting your ex. But speaking realistically, if you do give into this urge, make sure you forgive yourself and make sure to make every effort not to do it again. Relapse is sometimes an inevitable part of recovery from addiction. Being consumed with shame or guilt will only pull you deeper into the addiction. That's why it's so important to radically accept your craving to your addiction to this person; these cravings may always be there.

The point is not to eradicate craving but not to act on your craving. It will get easier. Also, No Contact consists of no social media stalking. So if you're still on Facebook looking through his or her pictures and statuses, don't be fooled. You're still engaging. You're still placing your hand back in the fire and you're taking the risk that you'll endure even more trauma. Write this letter for you and you alone. No expectations. No censoring. No people pleasing. Just your authentic voice.

Under no circumstances should you MEET with your ex. Sending angry texts is not wise, but it sure beats meeting up with your ex, begging him to take you back and degrading your self-esteem. You may have a "revenge" or "getting back together" fantasy associated with meeting up, but most likely you will just end up feeling more used and debased. Follow the Minimum Harm Principle: sit on your hands if you wish to contact him, and if you fall off the wagon, just get back on it and quick.

Don't use a slip-up to do more damage to yourself and your wellbeing. There may be many things you want to say to your ex, and sometimes falling off the wagon and expressing yourself can also be a healthy way to let it out before permitting yourself to move on. The process works differently for everyone, but remember that you should only allow yourself to fall off the wagon once or twice. Set a limit and stick to it.

Here are some tips to maintain No Contact:

- Make a list of consequences of contacting him (or her) if you need to, including the feelings you might feel if he rejects you or doesn't respond, the satisfaction you're giving his ego, and the fact that you're chasing after someone who is not worthy of you.
- Have a person you can call, text or e-mail when you get the urge to break No Contact. If that person is not available, go to a supportive forum for abuse survivors and write on there instead. Many people will be struggling with the same urge and will be sure to convince you otherwise. Even if they don't convince you, they will give you a supportive and validating space to vent, a better use of your energy than wasting your words on someone who mistreated you.

- Engage in a pleasurable activity and distract yourself (watching tv, going out for a run). Give yourself at least an hour's length of space before you act on any impulses or urges.
- Instead of contacting your ex, write that unsent letter to him and say everything you have left to say. If feeling the urge to share it, read it aloud to a trusted friend or therapist.
- Delete your ex-partner off your phone and all social networking sites (this is important because you do not want to be stalking him and keeping tabs on his relationship status). Delete or hide photos off your computer and social media feeds if you have to, in order to give yourself space from this person and anything that reminds you of him.

Remember: when things seem out of control, make the decision to TAKE back control. You ARE capable to making changes that transform your circumstances. You have the power to change the direction of your life. No Contact is a crucial way to do so.

Let yourself grieve. It's better to face the grief head-on rather than have it fester within you and eventually explode. Of course, when you're at work or school, you won't be able to express your grief openly. So you have to create your own space and time outside of these arenas to express your grief.

Not all grief can be expressed in a safe space, however. You might find yourself shedding tears on public transportation or in a bar when that special song you two enjoyed together plays. You may even break down in front of a friend when talking about the break-up. This is normal, and the important part is that you allow yourself to feel the grief. Crying manifests the internal struggle we're having and gives us some temporary relief.

Think of each sobbing session as medicine – it's a sign that you're brave and strong enough to confront your emotions, and it will benefit you in the long run because you won't have to grieve as much later. However, you may return to this grieving stage at a later time. Still, it won't be the raw, painful grief you feel right after the break-up. Don't set a time limit on your grief. Accept it and let it be. Now that you're free of someone who may have set limits on what you were supposed to feel previously, you can finally own and honor your emotions without feeling ashamed.

Treat yourself. You deserve it. The grieving process can be just as rewarding as it is painful. You can treat yourself to a massage, a yoga class, a dance class, or an extra long marathon of your beloved television series. This all goes back to the positive reinforcement schedule we were discussing earlier. It doesn't matter what you do, so long as it is something you personally find pleasurable and something you might not normally give yourself permission to do. Invest in yourself during this time because it is so worth it and you are so worth it.

You deserve some comfort during this time of grief. I remember during a past break-up, I went to my favorite massage place and I got a medicinal massage that soothed both my mind and spirit. I allowed myself to indulge in this because I knew I deserved it. It reminded me that life is pleasurable with or without a relationship, and this is an essential habit you are going to have to develop while single.

Surround yourself with caring people. Don't go through this process all alone. You may have only a few close friends or dozens. The point is, choose the people you surround yourself with wisely. This means choosing someone who is a good listener, compassionate, validating but also someone who will give you tough love when you need it. Maybe you don't have one person who is all of these things: that's okay. You can have multiple people to fulfill your different needs: the friend who takes you out and forces you to have fun, the friend who listens to you vent and cry at night, the friend who talks sense into you during your breaking points. If you're lucky, you'll find this all in one or two people, but realistically, it may take a village (and a therapist!). Using professional support to navigate any triggers, flashbacks, nightmares or other symptoms of trauma you may be experiencing is also very important.

You may already have an intuition about which friends will help you and which friends will harm you during this process (these are the self-absorbed or negative friends we talked about previously who don't even deserve your time or energy, so after your break-up, I'd advise letting them go). Don't choose these friends to talk to. In fact, avoid them during this time. You don't need their negative energy depressing your spirits even more.

Take care of your health. As we talked about earlier, self-care is holistic which means you have to tend to your physical body too. If you're not eating enough, find creative ways to make sure you do get what you need. Drink protein shakes or eat nutrition bars. Eat smaller meals throughout the day. If you're eating too much, try writing down what you eat every day and find ways to decrease your portions. Or find "healthy" treats that you can indulge in without overwhelming your body with unhealthy things that will leave you feeling more stressed out and drained. Find gentle forms of exercise and restorative yoga that you can do if you're not feeling up to more energetic forms of exercise during this time. Daily, thirty-minute walks in nature can also be helpful because it boosts our serotonin levels while also replenishing our bodies.

THE BREAK-UPVERSERY – ONE OR TWO MONTHS AFTER THE BREAKUP

You've done it. You've survived a month or two of enduring No Contact (or falling off the wagon and getting back on), erasing your ex from cyberspace, crying your eyes out, treating yourself to pleasurable activities, and reconnecting with the friends who truly do care about you and want to help you. You've even reached what I call the "Break-UpVersery," exactly one or two months after the date of the break-up. This is a milestone and it should be celebrated. But not by breaking No Contact. Not by hooking up with random strangers. Not by drinking yourself to sleep, either.

By breathing in and out. And enjoying your alone time. Wait...what? Perhaps you thought that the grieving process WAS the "alone time," but it's unfortunately not that simple. You might be discouraged when you discover that one or two months of grieving doesn't necessarily mean "Go forward to the next relationship." In fact, the grieving process is only the first step in your healing.

We've all heard the cliché that to get over someone you have to get under someone else. But actually, you may harm yourself by doing this. Not only are you using someone else as an emotional sponge to absorb all of your insecurities (which never works), you aren't allowing yourself the time and space you actually require to reflect on your past relationships, deal with toxic habits, and learn from your experiences.

If you're the type to jump from one relationship to another without much of a pause in between, this break-up could be your epiphany moment or turning point. It could be the moment to break the pattern of entering unhealthy relationships once and for all. Take on the privilege of being single for a while.

That's right. Being single is a privilege. Maybe you've never looked at it that way, because we're socialized to think that coupledom is the ultimate goal of a successful life. But singlehood truly is a privilege if you learn to look at it through the appropriate lens. If you are someone who anticipates or hopes of being married in the future, recognize that being single is the only time you will have to develop yourself without anyone or anything holding you back. You can develop spiritually, emotionally, physically, and professionally. You might even meet the right person during this journey because you will be focusing on being your best self and exuding positive energy, but that will just be the icing on the cake. It's not the actual goal. The goal is to fulfill your potential and grow tremendously.

The real pleasure will be in applying all the things you learned in the first half of the book, along with the personal development strategies you'll learn in the remaining chapter. You will focus on weeding out unhealthy friendships, creating enjoyable hobbies, working on your goals and dreams, and enjoying your life being your authentic self. And when you do find the right person, you will be ready for him or her, because you will have accepted and loved yourself to the point where you will only choose someone who ADDS immense value to your life. Not someone who brings you down, but someone you will actively CHOOSE to have in your life because it simply adds more happiness – not because it is the source of your happiness. The source of your happiness will remain YOU.

Ultimately, you are the sole judge on when it's time to move onto the next relationship. Just remember: Trust your instincts. They are gold. If you hear a voice inside you telling you that you're not ready, or your body is overwhelmed with a feeling of panic, LISTEN TO THAT VOICE.

As women, we are socialized not to listen to ourselves. We're told to constantly look for society to tell us what to do, think, feel, wear, and look like. We forget that our instincts come from a source that is beyond rational thinking and beyond other people's suggestions. Our intuition knows us better than we know ourselves and the world. Develop a relationship with your intuition, do "insight" meditations where you simply listen to that voice within you and connect to the inner spirit that is meant to guide you in your decisions.

Would you rather continue to sabotage potentially good relationships with your lack of readiness while stringing someone else along, or would you rather wait, be patient with yourself, enjoy your alone time and give yourself time to heal? That healing time is completely essential regardless of whether or not you plan on having another relationship (and plans of course, can always change with circumstances).

Remember, if you choose a partner during a time when you're an emotional wreck, you'll most likely end up gravitating towards someone on your level. This has happened to me many times. The more emotionally unavailable you are, the more likely you will find a partner who mirrors you in toxic and unhealthy ways. The only difference will be that you will be so willing to work on it and invest in it because you want to prove you're loveable. It will be a devastating rejection when you realize they aren't willing to put in the same effort. The only reason you feel rejected by this unworthy person (and yes, this person is truly unworthy of your time or attention) is because you haven't worked on your own issues and taken the time to cultivate a healthier image of yourself and a more accurate portrait of your needs, boundaries, and values. So, remember to always look out for the red flags when you start dating again, if you do start dating again.

REMEMBER: THERE IS A DISTINCTION BETWEEN VICTIM-BLAMING AND OWNING OUR AGENCY

Victim-blaming is a touchy subject for many survivors, and rightfully so. Survivors of emotional and/or physical abuse are sickened by victim-blaming. I am, too. Why wouldn't we be? We have been in relationships where we were constantly gaslighted, mislead, invalidated and mistreated. The last thing we need is the outside world blaming us for not leaving soon enough, or for getting into the relationship in the first place. It's a whole other degree of invalidation that survivors simply don't need. It hurts us even more that the world refuses to acknowledge how difficult it is to leave an abusive relationship when you're in the midst of it, because you're experiencing so much cognitive dissonance that you don't even know whether to trust your own perceptions and realities. Abusive relationships severely hinder our perceived agency, overwhelm us with a sense of learned helplessness, and make it difficult for us to navigate the seemingly impossible constraints imposed by these toxic relationships.

I wholeheartedly understand this, and sympathize. However, I want to draw a distinction between victim-blaming versus acknowledging that we do we have the power to change our lives. I feel this gets lost somewhere in our resistance to concepts that may challenge us to evaluate and examine ourselves during the healing process or may appear to be blaming us for the abuse but can actually challenge us to move forward towards self-improvement and fulfillment. I feel, as both victims and survivors, we have a tendency to belittle or demean any concept, idea or helping resource that tells us to also look inward when unraveling our own relationship habits. I understand why this would be the case – we might perceive these resources as being patronizingly ignorant. We might think these resources are telling us that we somehow asked for the abuse, or that we attracted it. Some resources are in fact victim-blaming, but we have to learn to distinguish between what is victim-blaming versus what is encouraging us to own our own agency. Only when we learn this distinction can we also own our "surviving" and thriving status as well as our legitimate victimization by the toxic partner.

I know that there are many survivors out there who had never experienced interacting with a narcissist or a sociopath before they had this experience. They feel strongly about the fact that their relationship patterns were healthy before they met the narcissist or sociopath. Still, even for those survivors, we can learn a lot about our own strengths (and weaknesses) from this experience. Not because those weaknesses justify the abuse, but because all human beings have imperfections and vulnerabilities, and emotional predators tend to prey on these.

If we tend to enjoy flattery and equate it with genuine care or love (which most people do!), we now have the power to change that perspective and acknowledge that the next time someone tries to excessively "love-bomb" or idealize us, our experiences have taught us that it is not necessarily equivalent to sincerity, and that it may actually be a red flag. Acknowledging that we have the ability to now see red flags and recognize them, is not victim-blaming, but owning our agency and ability to protect ourselves.

It is true that emotionally abusive people can hide behind masks for so long that we may never know we're with one until years later. However, that is why it is so important to create strong boundaries early on so that no one person can dominate your life. That is why it is so important to spend time alone before you enter new relationships, to get accustomed to enjoying yourself, so that should these red flags come up, you know you have the choice to leave, and the threat of being lonely will not stop you.

For survivors who do have a pattern of getting involved with pathologically unstable men and remaining with them, I do not believe it is blaming yourself to try to understand yourself better as a result of this. Whether it's acknowledging that you had a narcissistic parent that may have influenced your own relationship with a narcissist or whether it's examining how the relationship took a toll on you, it really is beneficial to always reflect upon what happened, how it affected you, how it may have triggered past traumas.

This reflection shouldn't be confused with blaming the victim or saying that the victim "wanted" the abuse – it's about recognizing the impact of the trauma bonds that kept us tethered to this person while still maintaining our ability to heal ourselves. It's about recognizing any insecurities or any people-pleasing behavior that may be holding us back from fully healing and owning our full potential while knowing that we were unfairly mistreated. It's also about acknowledging our strengths – our empathy, compassion, the beautiful qualities of humanity that the Narcissist or Sociopath lacks, and recognizing that these were taken advantage of.

Whether you call the patterns of an emotionally abusive relationship codependency (a controversial term) trauma bonding, Stockholm Syndrome, in my (humble) opinion, isn't as important as acknowledging that you cannot change or control the pathology of the other person, but that you can make positive changes in your own life by initiating and maintaining No Contact, engaging in taking care of yourself fully and holistically during the healing process and afterwards, and pursuing your dreams while moving forward. This is about owning our story and owning our agency. This is not saying that anything the Narcissist or Sociopath did to you was your fault; not at all. It is saying that you are STRONGER than what he or she did to you, and that you will use this opportunity to reflect, return any blame to your perpetrator, and acknowledge that in the future, you have the power (and now the resources) to walk away from what no longer serves you.

The reason I am writing this note is because I don't want our resistance to victim-blaming (a perfectly legitimate protest) to be confused with not acknowledging our remaining agency and power, something we felt was threatened or even lost completely due to the abuser's control over us. We do not have the power to determine the terrible things people do to us; but we do have the agency and power to turn to constructive outlets for healing.

We do not have the power to stop ourselves from being a victim of a crime; but we do have the agency and power to help other survivors by sharing our story. We do not have the power to change a narcissist or sociopath or control the degree to which they abuse us; but we do have the power to take the time to heal and not enter a new relationship until we're fully ready to do so. Our choices still exist. We are simultaneously victims and survivors; we have regained our agency and power from the abusive relationship and this enables us to thrive and heal in ways we must recognize and acknowledge.

Our interactions with narcissists give us an immense opportunity to look at what needs to be healed within us (whether these wounds were created via the relationship, past traumas or both), what boundaries we need to be more firm about (for example, not letting a partner communicate with us only via text and stay in contact 24/7 can protect us from what is likely the love-bombing from an emotionally unavailable con artist), and what values we hold most dear (if someone doesn't share our values of loyalty, fidelity, and integrity, we now know these are deal-breakers even if we tried to negotiate this in the past). We may have lost our sense of agency and power when we're struggling in a relationship with Narcissists or Sociopaths, but now we can take back the control.

These experiences remind us what is most important: self- love and self-care. It is not victim-blaming to look at what positive changes we can make in our lives to better ourselves, nurture and heal ourselves from the abuse we've endured. Not because we're "attracting" or "asking" for these people in any way, but because we DID in fact experience harmful relationships with them. We are not perfect, but we did not in any way deserve or invite the abuse. We can improve ourselves without having to blame ourselves. This means that we have to be proactive about healing without victim-blaming. There IS a distinction, and there is power in acknowledging that distinction.

HIT THE BOOKS

Being single is the optimal time to hit the books because you have extra time to yourself to breathe, relax and reflect. During my break-ups, I was privileged to have numerous resources on my path to self-discovery and reflection through self-help and self-improvement books. The great thing about breaking up is that so many people have been through break-ups in almost every form and level of trauma possible, so there's plenty of insight out there. It would be shameful if I didn't share these treasures with someone reading my book. Like I said earlier, it takes a village. Only reading "one" book won't help you – but reading multiple books will. You always need different perspectives, styles, and different books will meet your needs at different times. I've categorized them in a way I hope you find helpful, organizing them by theme to cater to your specific needs.

SELF-IMPROVEMENT & RELATIONSHIPS

Mr. Unavailable and the Fallback Girl by Natalie Lue – Natalie Lue changed my life. A friend recommended her blog, Baggage Reclaim (visiting her blog is also a must: http://baggagereclaim.co.uk), to me and once I read it, I felt like I was reading my life story. I felt like the "Fallback Girl," the one who treated herself like an option and chased emotionally unavailable men.

Natalie's insights about the tendency to try to nurse these men back to decent people struck a serious chord within me. This is a must-read book if you have a pattern of chasing emotionally unavailable men, if you've ever encountered one and got screwed over, or even if you're just trying to figure out whether YOU'RE emotionally available enough for a healthy relationship, because like often attracts like. I recommend reading both the book and the blog; both will have tremendous insight for almost every situation you could think of. The support network of BR readers and their comments will also help you realize that you are not alone – far from it.

Welcome to Your Crisis: How to Use the Power of Crisis to Create the Life You Want by Laura Day - Wonderful book on ways to reimagine and channel your crisis into transformation. I found the exercises in this book incredibly helpful for learning more about my strengths, talents and the multiple ways my crisis could be transformative.

Practical Intuition by Laura Day - Laura Day is a practicing intuitive and she addresses practical ways to tune into the intuition we often ignore or repress when we're with emotionally abusive people. This book is great for anyone who has rationalized away inappropriate behavior, broken their own boundaries for others and stopped listening to the inner voice meant to protect them.

The Seven Spiritual Laws to Success by Deepak Chopra – This is A MUST READ! One of the best books I've read so far on the law of attraction and achieving your dreams. It is intricate, beautifully written and full of the positive energy you'll require to propel you forward.

GRIEVING

Getting Past Your Breakup by Susan Elliot – Elliot is a grief counselor who used her many breakups to explore the process of grieving in the event of a traumatic loss. She jumped from relationship to relationship until one huge relationship ended and she realized she had to deal with the grief of ALL of her past relationships in addition to her most recent one. This was the powerhouse of breakup books for me. Elliot gives you numerous practical worksheets and tasks to work with to grieve properly, to stick to No Contact, and get past your breakup by making it a productive time for healing and reevaluating. Her book provides numerous insights into the grieving process and how it works cyclically rather than in phases.

NO CONTACT

The No Contact Rule by Natalie Lue is a must. It's the foundational book for learning the rules of no contact, even in circumstances where it seems impossible. It also outlines the reasons why pursuing men after the breakup is essentially a waste of time and energy you could be using to move forward and work on yourself.

MOVING ON

It's Called a Breakup Because It's Broken by Greg Behrendt and Amiira Ruotola-Behrendt. Husband and wife team up to write a tongue-in-cheek breakup book with just the right dose of tough love and humor. If that's not adorable I am not sure what is. Greg is the author of the popular He's Just Not That Into You book, which, while helpful, was not as helpful to me as this book. Mostly because I think women deserve the reasons why they shouldn't be into certain men rather than the other way around, and this is exactly what you'll get from this book. Greg and Amiira use both tough love and encouragement (along with some pretty horrific breakup stories from around the world) to make you pick yourself up and start living again.

This is something you must read, especially if you feel you can't move on.

SELF-LOVE

The Single Woman – Life, Love and a Dash of Sass by Mandy Hale – Creator of the infamous The Single Woman twitter feed, Hale tells the story of experiencing her relationship with an emotionally unavailable man as well as a tale of her own horrific abuse. She reintroduces the idea of the single woman as a woman of strength and the single status as a source of celebration rather than grief.

Madly in Love With Me: The Daring Adventure of Becoming Your Own Best Friend by Christine Arylo – This book has wonderful exercises on how to cultivate all aspects of what Arylo calls the "self-love tree." If you're looking to understand what self-love truly entails, this is the place to start.

Love Yourself Like Your Life Depends On It by Kamal Ravikant focuses on the mantra "love yourself" and how it can transform your entire life. Start with this book if nothing else.

If you'd like to learn more about narcissistic abuse and covert emotional violence, I also recommend reading my other books, *Becoming the Narcissist's Nightmare* and *Power: Surviving and Thriving After Narcissistic Abuse*.

Remember this: you are now free of the abuse and pain of the past. You are now free to live a better life without someone toxic by your side. Free to find true love within yourself and in the future, with someone worthy of you. Stay strong, because you can channel the pain from the past into self-empowerment and victory.

HELPFUL ONLINE TOOLS AND RESOURCES:

Self-Care Haven for Survivors
(My Blog on Emotional Trauma and Recovery)
http://www.selfcarehaven.wordpress.com

Joseph Clough's Be Your Potential podcast
http://josephclough.com/blog?category=Podcast

Psychopath Free Forum for Emotional and Physical
Abuse Survivors:
https://www.psychopathfree.com/forum.php

Let Me Reach, Surviving Narcissistic Abuse by Kim
Saeed:
http://letmereach.com/

After Narcissistic Abuse (ANA)
http://afternarcissisticabuse.wordpress.com/

Signs That You May Have an Abusive Boyfriend by
Natalie Lue
http://www.baggagereclaim.co.uk/signs-that-you-may-have-
an- abusive-boyfriend/

The National Domestic Violence Hotline:
http://www.thehotline.org/

7 SINGLEDOM: HEALING AND LOVING YOURSELF

Being single and rediscovering yourself can be an empowering period in your life, but there's no need to sugarcoat it: it can also be incredibly painful, confusing, heart-wrenching and depressing at times. The reasons?

Society views singledom as an involuntary, torturous status and women specifically internalize this view from early on. It doesn't help that women are socialized to depend on relationships for their self-worth, and studies confirm that women do indeed have more of an interpersonal orientation than men, tend to ruminate more, and seek more reassurance of their worth from their relationships (Winstead and Sanchez, 2012).

Despite the divorce rate in America being incredibly high and a drastic reshaping of the traditional nuclear family over the past decades, people still equate "being single" with "being lonely" or assume that someone wants a relationship even if they're not currently in one.

Most of your friends may have boyfriends or husbands by a certain age and you feel this adds pressure, expectations and even a sense of something

missing from your own life. Depending on the culture you come from, you may also face familial pressures to marry and have children by a certain age. The pressure to be part of a couple is thus immense. You may have friends who are in long-term relationships or are already married depending on your age (even if you are young, you still may have friends in either situation). This creates some difficulty in your own healing process, because, inevitably, we are human and we want what we don't have.

When we witness the tender moments, declarations of love and vows, we can also feel a sense of sadness that we aren't experiencing these ourselves, even if we are happy for others. This feeling is completely normal, but it's important to not let the game of comparison overwhelm you into thinking that you'll be single forever if your goal is to eventually find a healthy relationship. There isn't something wrong with you if you are single while all your friends are hitched; your journey will not be the same as the journey of others.

Many people don't cope well with being single and turn to self-destruction or maladaptive behaviors to fill a void within themselves. We observe the behavior of others and model that behavior. When we observe our friends hooking up with men, dating multiple men, moving from one man to the next, we believe that's also the way we should cope with a break-up. I don't condemn anyone for doing these things in general – in fact, I encourage having a period of exploration in your life because a lot of people MISS OUT on new experiences before they rush into coupledom and marriage.

This ripe period is known as emerging adulthood and should be taken advantage of (Arnett, 2000).

Characterized by instability, exploration, risk-taking and change, experiencing emerging adulthood gives us the opportunity to test the waters and form our identity in creative and exciting ways; this can range from dating different people to exploring different countries or career paths. Without experimentation and exploration, how else would you find out who you are? It is your choice to lead WHATEVER lifestyle you wish so long as it fulfills you and your needs.

However, I don't recommend this behavior **immediately** after a breakup or as a result of a breakup because it encourages a pattern of "numbing" yourself to the pain of the breakup and not letting yourself heal. By using people as emotional sponges, we just slow ourselves down in the healing process. We hurt others and ourselves by clinging to people who are otherwise not compatible with us – often attracting emotionally unavailable people because we haven't given ourselves the time to work on our own emotional availability. Immediate gratification, while tempting and sometimes useful in certain circumstances, is not usually the way to go when it comes to a breakup: being single for a while IS. Learning to be happy single is essential if you ever hope to be in a healthy, lasting and happy relationship with someone else.

THE IMPORTANCE OF NO CONTACT WITH ABUSERS WHILE SINGLE

I talked about No Contact in the last chapter but I want to mention it again for those who are survivors of abusive relationships. If you are now single and free from your abuser, it is very important that you remain No Contact with the ex-partner or at least minimal contact if you share children with this partner.

What No Contact is and what it isn't

No Contact (NC) is not a game or a ploy to get a person back into our lives; this technique has been misrepresented in many dating books and blogs. We should not desire to have people who have mistreated us back into our lives. On the contrary, No Contact is a way to remove this person's toxic influence so we can live happier, healthier lives while cultivating our authentic self and minimizing people- pleasing. As shown by the image above, No Contact is the key that locks out that person from ever entering our heart, mind, and spirit in any palpable way again.

Why We Establish No Contact in the Context of Abusive Relationships

We establish No Contact for a number of reasons, including preserving a healthy mind and spirit after the ending of a toxic, unhealthy or abusive relationship or friendship. NC gives trauma bonds, bonds which are created during intense emotional experiences, time to heal from abusive relationships. If we remain in constant contact with the toxic person, we will only reinvigorate these trauma bonds and form new ones. No Contact also gives us time to grieve and heal from the ending of an unhealthy relationship or friendship without reentering it. Most of all, we establish No Contact so that toxic people like Narcissists and Sociopaths can't use hoovering or post-breakup triangulation techniques to win us back over. By establishing No Contact, we essentially remove ourselves from being a source of supply in what is clearly a non- reciprocal, dysfunctional relationship.

How to Execute No Contact Effectively

Full No Contact requires that we do not interact with this person in any manner or through any medium. This includes in-person and virtual contact. We must thus remove and block the person from all social media networks, because the toxic person is likely to attempt to trigger and provoke us through these mediums by posting updates on their lives post-breakup. We must also block them from messaging or calling us or contacting us via e-mail. Avoid the temptation to find out about the person's life via a third party or other indirect way. Remove triggering photos, gifts and any other reminders from your physical environment and from your computer.

Always refuse any requests to meet up with this person and ignore any places the person frequents. Should the person stalk or harass you by other means and you feel comfortable taking legal action, please do so. Your safety comes first. If you are in a situation where you must remain in contact with an ex-partner for legal issues or because of children, keep in low contact (minimum communication) and use the Gray Rock method of communication if this person has narcissistic (NPD) or antisocial (ASPD) traits. You can find a link to more information about the Grey Rock method at the end of this chapter.

I also highly recommend cutting contact with the friends of the abusive ex-partner if possible as well by also removing them from your social media sites. I understand you may have established great friendships with these people during the course of your relationship but if you did date a narcissist or sociopath, he or she has likely staged a smear campaign against you and you will not get any validation or support from these people.

Unfortunately, the narcissistic harem or fan club is ultimately convinced by the illusion and false self of the charming manipulator. Think of your ex-partner's "friends" (more like supply) as being kept in a perpetual idealization phase with no discard - they are not likely to believe your accounts of the abuse and may even be used by the narcissist or sociopath to hoover, triangulate, trigger or manipulate you in some way. It's best to cut ties with them completely and create your own support network that is separate from the abuser.

Stick to No Contact

If NC is a struggle for you, there many ways to ensure that you stick to it. Make sure you have a weekly schedule filled with pleasurable, distracting activities, such as spending time with friends, going to a comedy show, getting a massage, taking long walks, and reading helpful books such as The No Contact Rule by Natalie Lue.

Take care of your physical and mental well-being by exercising daily, establishing a regular sleep schedule to keep your circadian rhythms in balance, doing yoga to help strengthen your body and relieve stress, as well as engaging in a daily meditation practice of your choice. I offer a Healing Meditation for Emotional Abuse Survivors on my YouTube channel, and Meditation Oasis is also an excellent resource for guided meditations. You may also experiment with alternative healing methods such as Reiki, acupuncture, or aromatherapy. For more information on alternative healing methods, I highly recommend the tools for healing section on Kim Saeed's blog, Let Me Reach, the link to which you can find at the end of this chapter.

Do yourself a favor and look up online forums that relate to unhealthy and toxic relationships; joining such a forum ensures that you have a community and support network that enables you to remain NC and support others who are struggling just like you. It will also help validate some of the experiences that you went through during the friendship or relationship with people who've been there.

Do not resist your grief during this process, because you will have to face it at some point. The more you resist negative thoughts and emotions, the more they'll persist - it's a fact. Learn how to accept your emotions and accept the grieving process as an inevitable part of the healing journey. I recommend trying the grieving exercises and abiding by the No Contact rules in the book Getting Past Your Breakup, written by certified grief counselor Susan Elliot.

Most of all, develop a healthier relationship with your cravings to break NC by practicing radical acceptance and mindfulness to the present moment. Remember that relapse may be an inevitable part of the addiction cycle and forgive yourself if you do break NC at any point. After practicing this self-compassion and forgiveness, you must get back on the wagon after falling off of it. Track your urges to break NC in a journal to curb acting upon the urges. Make sure that before you act on any urge, you give yourself at least an hour to collect yourself. It will get easier once you realize that breaking NC often bears no rewards, only painful learning experiences.

Why We Remain No Contact

The ending of an unhealthy relationship often leaves us reeling and feeling unable to cope. Even though we logically know we did not deserve the abuse or mistreatment, we may be tempted to stray from this when our emotions get a hold of us. Trauma bonds often keep us tethered to the abuser, as well as other factors such as codependency, low self-esteem, feelings of low worth, which may have been instilled in us from the abusive patterns within the relationship or may have kept us in the relationship in the first place.

No Contact is a space for healing and reviving yourself, apart from the belittling influences of your former partner or friend. It is an opportunity for you to detach completely from the toxic person while moving forward with your life and effectively pursuing your goals. It enables you to look at the relationship honestly and productively from the realm of your own intuition, perceptions, emotions and thoughts, apart from the gaslighting or abuse of the former partner.

Remember that anyone who has treated you with anything less than respect does not deserve to be in your life, so NC helps you to resist the temptation to invite them back into your life in any manner or form. Many survivors find it helpful to track their progress on a calendar, blog or journal. You should celebrate and take note of your NC progress, as it is both a challenging and rewarding path to self-empowerment.

By establishing No Contact, you are ultimately staging your own victory and exploring your strengths, talents and new freedom with more ease. I invite you take the first steps to recovery and success by challenging yourself to at least 30 days of NC if you are doing it for the first time. This will provide a detoxifying period where you can start to heal in a protective space of self-care and self-love, enabling your mind and body to repair itself from the abuse. Then, utilize the resources I've mentioned here in order to maintain NC and purge your life of the toxic influences you were once tethered to.

HEALING AND TIME FOR ABUSE SURVIVORS

If you are both single and a survivor of trauma and abuse, recovery becomes much more complex than just embracing your single status. It might even mean grappling with the effects of PTSD, Stockholm Syndrome, trust issues, low self-esteem and depression, all of which can make us feel psychologically tethered to our abusers even after the ending of such a relationship.

Survivors of abuse and emotional trauma have a special and significant relationship with time. I've heard numerous stories that end with, "I can't believe I wasted this amount of time on this person," or, "These years of my life have been wasted!" We constantly question how much "longer" it will take before we are fully healed from our past experiences and whether or not we are ever fully healed. It is a painful realization when we recognize that we've given our precious time and energy into something that deeply wounded us.

Sometimes it takes a horrifying diagnosis or the ending of a relationship to force us to reflect on the time we have left, but we can be mindful of the present right now, at this very instant. Although we cannot go back in time to change the way we've spent it, it's important that we stay mindful of the time that we still possess, in the here and now.

In order to spend our time more constructively, we must do the following:

Allocate more time for healing rather than ruminating. Excessive rumination may be the initial response to the ending of an abusive relationship or after a significant trauma. Survivors of trauma may suffer from symptoms related to PTSD or acute stress disorder, like numbing, dissociative symptoms, recurrent nightmares, flashbacks, hypervigilance and intrusive thoughts. While it's extremely important to be patient with ourselves and not rush the healing process, it's also necessary to make active changes in our lives in order to make progress.

For the sake of our mental health, addressing our painful emotions and assessing what happened is necessary to moving forward, and we eventually come to the stage where we have to set aside time for what is necessary to heal ourselves. That means being proactive by seeking out professional help, setting boundaries such as low or No Contact with an abusive ex-partner, maintaining a strong support network and engaging in self-care that nourishes our body, spirit and mind.

CHALLENGE: Set a "time limit" for excessive ruminations. If you find yourself ruminating for three hours a day over a particular situation for example, set the time limit to one hour and then spend the rest of the time doing something else like exercising, working on a project, watching a favorite television show, meeting with a friend to do something fun, or writing a poem.

You may still have distracting thoughts during that time, but at least you will be spending more time doing an activity that benefits you rather than spending more time than is necessary reevaluating scenarios that you've revisited too many times. Whenever these intrusive thoughts come up, try not to feed them. Step back, observe, and radically accept them, just as they are. Engage in pleasurable distractions or cross another thing off your to- do list. Allow yourself the right to feel all of your emotions, but do not get stuck and permit them to hold you back from enjoying your life.

It's inevitable that we will think about the trauma and that we will have strong feelings about it. There is absolutely nothing wrong with that - it's a normal response to trauma. I make this suggestion to end excessive ruminations not to invalidate the legitimate feelings and thoughts about trauma that may surface, but to acknowledge that your time here on earth is precious and finite, and you want to spend it in a balanced way.

If you want to move forward, spending excess time overanalyzing situations rather than actively engaging with your life will only deter you from living your life the way it was meant to be led. You must spend some time assessing your trauma, but don't forget to spend time healing from it as well. Take breaks to relax, work on your goals and live life. This goes back to maintaining that delicate balance between owning both our status as survivor as well as our agency.

Take the time to pursue your unique destiny. In *The Seven Spiritual Laws of Success*, Deepak Chopra speaks about the "law of dharma," which is the unique destiny we're meant to fulfill. Chopra argues that our "dharma," our "purpose in life," manifests best when tied to serving humanity and the larger world around us. We have to ask ourselves, how much time am I spending on cultivating this destiny? What do I do every day to serve humanity? Is my current job fulfilling me? Is there volunteer work or another line of work I can pursue to make better use of my talents? Is there a talent that I am wasting rather than sharing with my current efforts?

Every single one of us has something we can do to change the world while changing ourselves for the better. Whatever you may call it - destiny, dharma, mission or fate, start asking yourself today: what's yours?

CHALLENGE: Write down two or three talents or skills that you feel you haven't used in a while, or haven't used at all in public. Next to each one, write at least five things you can do to cultivate that talent. If possible, pay special attention to how that talent may serve others. These things can be big or small in the way they help others.

For example, if one of my hidden talents was photography, I could volunteer as a wedding photographer to capture the meaningful moments in my friends' wedding or start a project that involves taking photographs for a social cause I care about. If my hidden talent was nutrition and fitness, I could volunteer to teach fitness classes at a local community center or start a YouTube channel to help people to change their diets and lifestyles. If I had a great sense of humor, I might use it to regularly brighten someone's day or I might join an improv comedy group and participate in shows that entertain hundreds of people in need of their daily escape. If I had a passion for mental health and loved to write, I could start a self-help blog or write a self-help book (sound familiar?).

You get the picture. There are so many creative ways to use our talents and put them into use to serve humanity. In the midst of this exercise, you might even come across what you were meant to do all along. This is a better use of our time and it permits us to change the world rather than to focus on what we can't change - the past.

Enjoy and be mindful of the present moment. Be grateful for what you still have now in the present moment. From basic things like food, shelter, our vision, our ability to walk, to good friends, a stable job and access to health care and education. Cultivating this habit of lifelong gratitude brings us to a place of mindfulness that is beneficial to our health and appreciation of life. Remember: time spent on remorse detracts from time spent savoring what we still have. Nothing lasts forever, so focus on what is still here.

CHALLENGE: Start to replace unhelpful thoughts and cognitive distortions about the past with positive statements about the present. Whenever judgmental statements like, "I shouldn't have done this" or "I regret what happened," arise, replace it with, "I am grateful to have survived and learned from this experience."

If this is too difficult because of the extent of trauma you've endured, try to remind yourself of something you still have despite the trauma, like "I still have my health and that's what's most important" or "Now I have the freedom to pursue my dreams without interference." Not all "alternative thoughts" will work to diffuse ruminations over the past, but making a significant effort towards a more positive attitude about your life experience will help you become more resilient to obstacles in the long-run.

It is also helpful to keep a gratitude journal to remind yourself of all you have to be thankful for in this life. The more time you spend being grateful, the less time you spend being resentful and the more likely you'll have an increased sense of perceived agency in your life. You'll be more likely to see challenges as opportunities for growth rather than as dead ends, and more likely to constructively channel your life circumstances into life-changing awareness.

Put an end to other toxic interactions and potentially toxic relationships. These are the nonreciprocal, unfulfilling interactions or relationships that leave you emotionally drained and exhausted. They include: relationships that are past their expiration date, friendships that leave you feeling terribly about yourself, and other interactions with people who mistreat or disrespect you. This helps us to refocus our time on healthier, fulfilling relationships that will make us happier in the long-run.

Minimize the people-pleasing and cut ties with the people who don't accept you for who you are and who don't appreciate what you have to offer. This is necessary in order to make the most of our time and use it wisely. Should you need to maintain contact for whatever reason (for example, this could be a family member who you're forced to interact with on a weekly basis) it's important to at least significantly reduce the time and energy you spend interacting with this person or ruminating over your interactions with them.

CHALLENGE: Think of a person in your life who you've spent unnecessary time with and energy on recently. What can you do to reduce or end the interaction? Is there a way you can set a boundary so they don't contact you as often? Do you need to stand up to them and make it clear that you no longer want them in your life? Whatever you must do, do it now. Save yourself future pain and heartache of having to endure a relationship or friendship that isn't serving you by ending it now or detaching from it. These unfulfilling interactions only hold us back from the destiny we're meant to fulfill.

As survivors of trauma, our best bet is to keep moving forward and focus on our self-care and self-love. Only by doing so can we fulfill that destiny. As we learn to make better use of our time, we have to remember that healing is a lifelong journey. We may encounter several traumas on this journey, but recovery can be a productive process in that it makes us mindful of the time we've spent and the time we have left.

POSITIVE/ALTERNATE REBELLION

Another way to make the best use of our time is to rechannel our negative energy into positive or alternate rebellion, rebellion that doesn't harm you or others but still satisfies your need to resist your usual norms or rules for acting, thinking or behaving. By engaging in this type of rebellion, we substitute maladaptive and destructive behaviors with more "out-of-character" behavior that ends up benefiting us in the long-run.

Instead of moping around, self-destructing and thinking negatively about your lack of relationship status, these are healthier coping methods that ease your anxiety and fear over being single (assuming you have some) or your emotions about the traumas you've experienced. Here are some examples of how you can practice positive rebellion in your life:

Be happy for other couples and use them as a model for what you desire for your future relationships. This is another form of putting opposite action into practice and I know it's hard during the grieving process. People don't want to admit they're not as happy for their friends as they should be, or that they're jealous of the perfect couple smooching next to them. Or maybe you're the lucky one who finds it easy to be happy when you see a couple while you're going through a breakup – if so, major kudos.

However, if you're feeling twinges of jealousy and hurt whenever you see couples around, try to breathe and think to yourself, "This reminds me that love is possible." Whenever you witness a couple interacting lovingly, use it as an excuse to productively remodel your own understanding of love and relationships. What are the traits and behaviors that these couples engage in that inspire you? What do you see in them that you would like for your future relationship? Know that you are just as worthy of the love, empathy and respect they have – and their existence validates the fact that healthier love is possible.

If you're not feeling as idealistic, other helpful thoughts may be, "They look happy, but I am happy too. I can't compare my happiness with theirs; we are all different," or "I am sure I looked happy with my exes, too, but that didn't necessarily reflect what happened behind closed doors. Nobody is perfect."

You might find the last suggestion strange, as if it's a bitter thought, but really it's one that inserts some reality into the picture and challenges your cognitive distortion of All-or-Nothing thinking. You have to remember that you too, were once part of a couple. You too showed PDA (or perhaps you didn't), held hands, exchanged gifts, spent the holidays together. But you also fought with each other and struggled with fundamental incompatibilities. Recognize that even the happiest couples have problems and conflicts. Inject some realism and humanity to the perfect image couples seem to project, and you will find yourself more willing to be happy for these couples while keeping your head held high. Being happy for others is essential because bitterness holds us back and we simply won't get anywhere with our own goals if we're busy coveting what others have.

Don't forget to remember the benefits of being single even in the midst of all of this! Your happiness cannot be compared to anyone else's – you might have luxuries that some couples don't. There is nothing holding you back; maybe you rent your own apartment and have your own space; maybe you're independent, successful and thriving; now you have plenty of time and space to focus on yourself and invest only in yourself, your career and your travels. You now have more time to invest in quality friendships and professional networks. Your schedule is determined by you and you have absolutely no one else to consider – now that's what I call the ultimate freedom. There are so many ways to celebrate our single status rather than feeling down about it. And ironically, you'll find that the more comfortable you become being single and happy, the more the universe conspires against you (or with you?) to bring healthier potential partners into your life along the way. It's because you're radiating and exuding a newfound confidence – one that awesome potential partners and friends gravitate towards.

Find your true calling and stop being ashamed to follow it. Many dating books talk about how to be a woman worth pursuing by living a life filled with interesting adventures, hobbies and interests in order to attract quality men. Although the primary objective of these books is to find the guy, I want you to aim for...well, finding YOURSELF. Understanding what makes you tick.

What inspires you? What makes you feel good, happy, and strong? What is your secret passion or dream that you were too ashamed to explore because society or your family or friends or exes told you it wasn't possible or practical? Rebel against that idea in a positive way by pursuing that forbidden fruit.

For me, I had to come to terms with the fact that my passion and first love would always be writing, regardless of whatever else I pursued. I had multiple interests and talents, but it always came back to writing. Ultimately, following my dreams actually led me to a more fulfilling and more abundant life in ways I never thought possible – intellectually, spiritually, financially and emotionally. It was what I knew God put me on this earth to do, and because I followed my calling, I allowed myself to thrive. It was what made me excited about life. Your purpose can be found in the things you might not even expect. The things you take for granted. The talent you've hidden away in the pursuit of a "practical," socially acceptable career. If you feel lost, again, start by making a list of your passions. Then, based on these passions, create short-term and long-term goals for the year. Next, list the steps you need to achieve them. This will help you put things into perspective and will enable you to connect with your authentic desires as opposed to the desires society has imposed upon you.

Use your body as a powerful tool rather than as a site for self-destruction. As women, we are constantly being sold distorted images of what our bodies should and shouldn't look like. The objectification and sexualization of women in the media is a huge sociocultural factor that affects the development of eating disorders and negative body image among women. We're not told how to use our bodies to build strength and endurance; rather, we're told the best ways to lose belly fat. We lack confidence in our bodies and what they're capable of doing, because we take fitness classes for the sole reason of shedding that extra weight instead of for pleasure or enhancing our abilities.

It is no surprise then, that women are also more likely to self- injure or self-harm, while men externalize their rage and depression. Through societal and familial influences, their bodies are seen as property, not worthy of care or compassion. So how do we take back the ownership of our bodies and reignite the powerful ways we can reengage with them, without self-harm and without the rigid control of dietary restrictions?

While I was still in a relationship, I started taking fitness classes that made me feel so much more confident about myself and my body. This is a great way to relieve your stress especially if you're used to self-harm or other self-destructive behavior as a coping mechanism. It allows you to alternatively rebel by using your body as a strong force to be reckoned with rather than as a site of pain, dejection and deprivation. I took Zumba, Advanced Meditative Yoga, various Dance Cardio classes, Pilates and Cardio Kickboxing. After my breakup, I felt so blessed to be able to continue with these hobbies. They served as an amazing form of distraction and helped ground me emotionally and physically.

The fact is, I love dancing. I love meditating. I love kicking ass. So all of these passions, translated into action, really helped me build my self-esteem just as much as they enhanced my overall health. I also learned how to do things I never thought I could do: a headstand in yoga, increasing resistance in my Pilates poses with resistance machines or following difficult choreography with ease. If you feel doubtful that you can afford these types of classes, remember your friend Groupon, which always gives out deals for fitness.

Try new gyms and fitness centers without obligations, look online to see what gyms have trial memberships, and put yourself out there. You deserve it. If fitness isn't your thing, find other hobbies that interest you. Drawing, knitting, collecting, photography – don't consider these things leisurely activities you don't have the time for. Make the time. Remember, not all people are meant to stay in your life. But your life should eventually turn back to a stabilizing point after you've had time to process it and heal. This means you need to be able to return to the things you love to do. Feeling like your life hasn't changed outside of the relationship ending will help you move on faster and make you feel like the whole person you were before the breakup.

As a sidenote, if you want to learn more about harnessing your emotions into more productive outlets as an alternative to self-harm, I suggest reading *Live Through This: On Creativity and Self-Destruction*, edited by Sabrina Chap. This book showcases artists, writers and activists who epitomize the idea of turning to positive rebellion rather than self-harm.

Get in touch with your spiritual side. Rebel against the norm by trying out different techniques and learning more about a side you may not have cultivated or you may have abandoned in this era of scientific rationalism. There's always been that cliché that being alone enables us to connect to God in a more pure way, detached from secular desires. So travel in multiple ways. Visit different types of faith-based institutions and explore different religions and beliefs, if you're not already tied to a particular faith. Try Reiki healing or acupuncture. Attend an Energy Healing meetup. Read about manifestation, magic and seek out circles where powerful women use it to transform their lives – I am serious – if you're looking for some badass warrior goddess role models, you'll likely encounter them in spiritual circles where the divine feminine is celebrated. Even if you're not a believer in any of the things I've mentioned, it doesn't hurt to broaden your experience and learn about new things. Even if you're a stone-cold atheist and think all of these suggestions sound strange, chances are you've experienced something that has connected you to your sense of spirituality, greater purpose, or faith in some way or other during your lifetime.

Whether it was during a meditative silence or in the observation of a coincidence that felt more like a miracle or blessing, it felt life-changing and significant. Connecting with your spirituality is not New Age nonsense (although there's nothing with New Age things either). It's essential to our emotional well-being and sense of purpose in life that we connect with ourselves on a level that transcends our physical body. You don't have to follow a religion or a church to feel connected to the universe around you. A few moments of meditation each day, reflective writing or even reading spiritual-minded books can give you greater insight into a spiritual path you may sync with.

If you're finding it difficult to know where to even begin, start with a list of miracles or blessings your life has given to you and create a gratitude journal if you need to remind yourself of the good things still in your life every day. I know personally that I am a walking multi-faith poster child: I grew up in a Muslim family which stressed self- discipline and perfectionist tendencies; I visited both Christian churches and Islamic mosques; I have meditated in Buddhist centers; I also had a period where I was an agnostic on the verge of atheism until I let God into my life again. I don't subscribe to a specific religion, but I do believe in God, my greater purpose, and the power of prayer, writing and meditation - and that's my own version of spirituality. It's taken me a while to find this path and walk it with confidence.

Not everyone I knew understood my leap from atheism to God; and many didn't understand my inability to walk the path of Islam when I was raised that way, either. The point is, it doesn't matter what faith you subscribe to or what you believe in so long as you are in touch with something daily that helps you recognize your larger purpose and the importance of the world around you. It could be a mantra or a whole mindfulness program; it could be just the simple listing of miracles or an entire Gospel choir that brings you joy. Just have at least one thing that you can connect to that reminds you that you are not alone. Note: If you do want to believe in God, are seeking Him but are struggling to feel closer to Him, I recommend reading *Proof of Heaven: A Neurosurgeon's Journey into the Afterlife* by Eben Alexander III, a book that will make you think about the afterlife in new and unexpected ways.

Channel your aggression into productivity. Remember, being single can be a blessing if you make it so. This is your time to fully commit yourself to all your dreams and goals without interference, without a need to consider another person's interests or needs or wants. Use this time to be selfish (not a bad thing in this case) and schedule your time wisely. If you're in school, invest time to learn and study and excel. Challenge yourself and connect what you're learning to your greater purpose whenever possible.

Say you're a musician but you're studying something different because you want to expand your opportunities or because you have multiple talents – use everything you learn to serve you in other aspects of your life. Even learning to challenge yourself in class may motivate you to try something new in music. This will give you a sense of self-efficacy and knowledge that no one can take from you. It will also benefit your future career or, if you plan to pursue a higher level of schooling, your future academic career.

If you already have a full-time job, make sure it's something that is really benefiting you and not draining you. If it's benefiting you, go all out and use your energy to get that promotion or simply improve your skills whenever any opportunity arises. If it's draining you, look at other opportunities and explore your options. Just because you're in a specific position now doesn't mean you can't grow and move onto greener fields.

Make sure you leave some time for volunteering or working for a greater social cause – it will connect you back to the universe as you give to others, and it's SO much more productive than sitting at home stalking your ex on Facebook. You must do something to benefit the larger world around you. Strive to be a source of inspiration and positive influence for others. You have the potential to be an active agent for social change. Never waste that power.

Your life's purpose is larger than just your own needs and wants. Whether it's encouraging emotional support survivors online or working at the soup kitchen, get going. It's time to give back to those worthy of your "fixing" tendencies. Give back some energy to people who actually need and deserve it – rather than someone who made the active choice to no longer spend any energy on YOU. Remember, your destiny is not to stay with anyone who leaves you.

AN IMPORTANT NOTE FOR SELF-HARMERS:

Alternate rebellion techniques can be extremely useful for people who engage in self-harm. Self-harm, suicidal ideation and other parasuicidal behaviors are taboo topics, and they're ones I think need to be covered when we talk about self-care, precisely because they exist on the opposite side of the spectrum: self-destruction. The less we speak out about them, the more we stigmatize these topics and the more likely people who need help will be unlikely to seek it due to feelings of shame, alienation and isolation. You are not alone, and there is always someone out there who can listen to you and help you.

Since these are such heavy topics, I thought I would tackle it by beginning with the myths about self-harm and suicide before moving onto alternate rebellion tips for self-harm as well as other coping resources available to you. It is by first dispelling the popular myths that we can first begin to navigate the realities of it and offer solutions.

If you're currently having any suicidal thoughts or plans to harm yourself, please call the **National Suicide Prevention Hotline at 1-800-273-8255.**

I. THE MYTHS ABOUT SELF-HARM AND SUICIDE

1. Those who self-harm or who have suicidal ideation are selfish. This is simply not true. People who suffer from suicidal thoughts and urges are often suffering from an excess of pain and a lack of (internal and external) coping resources. If anything, self-harmers and those who have suicidal urges often feel like they impose a burden on loved ones by their very existence. Please try to remember this if you yourself self-harm or know someone who self-harms, because invalidating their emotional experiences may increase their perceived burdensomeness which can then increase their urges. Validation, a nonjudgmental stance and support are key when communicating with someone who engages in self-harm or expresses suicidal thoughts.

2. Those who self-harm or attempt suicide are just looking for attention. It's very possible that people who self-harm or attempt suicide are looking to receive help, but to minimize their pain as merely attention-grabbing techniques invalidates the real suffering they're going through and again perpetuates the myths that prevent them from getting the help they need in the first place. Yes, self-harmers can cry for help - but they do so because they actually need it. If you know someone who self-harms or struggles with suicidal thoughts/urges, try to show understanding and compassion in your approach rather than judgment. It can make a world of difference.

3. People who self-harm or attempt suicide are just unintelligent and weak. People who self-harm and have suicidal or parasuicidal tendencies might have mental health issues, but that does not have anything to do with their intelligence or strength. When we consider the role that trauma in the environment plays on early brain development, we should be more sensitive, compassionate and empathetic towards those who have suffered emotional trauma or who use self-harm as a coping mechanism.

Someone who self-harms or is suicidal is not any less intelligent or educated; he or she is struggling and needs help. Please do not promote this myth of "weakness" by judging this person as it takes an incredibly strong person to speak out, ask for help, and share his or her experience. Survivors of suicidal attempts or self-harm are actually immensely strong people; they have overcome a strong desire to self-destruct and/or die and are still thriving today. Remember that it takes a great deal of courage and strength to live and move forward when struggling with these thoughts and urges.

4. People who self-harm want to kill themselves. There is a distinction between suicide and self-harm, as well as the intent behind these two actions. As mentioned previously, people who self-harm use this as a maladaptive coping mechanism - the act of self-harm, paradoxically enough, essentially enables them to survive despite the pain they inflict upon themselves.

5. Suicidal ideation is the same as suicidal planning or action. Ideation involves thoughts and fantasies of suicide, but there is a difference between thinking about suicide and actually developing a plan.

Developing a plan places a person more at risk of actually acting upon their thoughts. Psychiatrists are taught to assess the difference with their clients and assess accordingly.

II. ALTERNATE REBELLION TIPS FOR SELF- HARM

1. Writing on your body in other ways. Use a red marker instead of a razor to mark yourself. Use a rubber band on your wrist and snap it every time you have the urge to self- harm. Punch a pillow to get the rage out. For those who are interested in body modification, former self-harmers like Demi Lovato have used tattooing as a creative art form to express pain through their body in positive ways. Instead of self-harming, consider getting a piercing or a tattoo that symbolizes something empowering to you.

2. Exercising as an empowering tool. Take a kickboxing class, a cardio kickboxing class, martial arts, self-defense or dance cardio class to get your heart pumping and to release endorphins in healthier ways. Learn to channel your aggression by propelling your body into movement. As mentioned before, exercise will not only will it help with the feelings of depression, helplessness and hopelessness, it will teach you to use your body as a vehicle for empowerment rather than as a site of pain and destruction.

3. Artistic expression. Write, draw, and create things instead of destroying yourself. Develop a weekly schedule that incorporates artistic expression and develop a habit of engaging in these outlets for expression. Not only will this promote healthier coping methods for when you experience extreme duress, you will be using your unique skills to showcase your talents and maybe even benefit the world around you if you choose to share them.

4. Meditate. Again, studies show that meditation literally changes gene expression which counter the "fight or flight" stress response, shapes the brain's neural networks to benefit the way our brain responds to stress and allocates attentional resources more efficiently. Meditation is a great stress reliever and can help you during times when you are feeling particularly impulsive and need to slow down, take a deep breath and refocus on the present moment. Develop a daily habit of meditating for at least ten minutes and use it whenever you feel overwhelmed by intrusive thoughts or urges to refocus your brain and bring it back to the present moment.

5. Rebel positively. Instead of harming yourself, do something that you otherwise might not do. You can make this a daily, weekly or monthly habit - whatever works for you, just so long as it satisfies your need to express yourself in healthier, productive ways. Speak your mind where you would normally stay quiet. Dress in a different way than what's expected of you. Do something fun instead of putting your usual responsibilities first. You can find more ideas in the "Ideas for Alternate Rebellion" link in the list below.

6. Tell someone. This is perhaps the most rebellious act because it means putting any shame, guilt or fear you have aside and telling the truth to someone you trust. If you feel comfortable doing so, confide in someone about what's happening (whether it's about your emotions or the act of self-harm itself, or both) instead of keeping it all in if you usually repress your thoughts and feelings. Having support is so important because it reminds you that you are cared for and worthy of love, respect and compassion.

By alternatively rebelling instead of engaging in self-harm, you also give that same love, respect and compassion to yourself. You deserve to live and you are needed in this world. You have a unique purpose. Never forget that on your journey.

ENTERING NEW RELATIONSHIPS

There will come a time in your life when you may start to date again and potentially even enter a new relationship. This can be both exciting and terrifying for young women who feel emotionally (and sometimes even physically) scarred by previously unhealthy relationships. While we can't ever be certain that a new relationship will work out, guarding ourselves to the point where we cannot even enjoy or engage in a new relationship is just as unhealthy as immersing ourselves in it to the point where we lose our identity and the independent lives we're struggling to create.

If you're ambivalent about entering a new relationship, most people will advise that you don't until you're fully ready. However, if you find yourself testing the waters anyway because you feel like the investment may be worth it and you are confident you can also work on yourself while simultaneously working on a new relationship, entering a new relationship can be a rewarding if not challenging experience.

Here's how to keep your head on your shoulders during this time and make sure you stick to your boundaries:

Don't give up your usual routine just for him or her. Of course, in the first few weeks of dating someone you really like, you may find yourself spending more time with him or her than with your usual activities and hobbies. That's perfectly fine, but make sure you balance it out. Don't abandon your friends and family during this time. This is crucial because while relationships don't always work out, your friends and family can serve as a more consistent support network through both happy and challenging times. Always remember that when you're dating or entering a relationship with someone new. Young women are socialized to give up everything in the pursuit of a significant other, and in the process, they tend to forget the people who have always been there for them regardless of their relationship status. Don't be one of those women — you will regret it. Continue doing the activities you love (ex: biking, yoga, dancing with friends) because these things will create a space for you to regroup and rejuvenate yourself, coming back to the person you're dating with a healthier mindset. You will also be communicating to your potential partner that you have a life outside of him or her, and are not dependent upon this relationship for happiness. This is extremely important because abusive partners tend to seek out people with codependent tendencies. By living and leading your own life, you are preventing yourself from becoming codependent.

Writing, Reflecting and Meditating can be crucial during this time. Let's face it; there are ebbs and flows in every relationship especially when the honeymoon phase starts to wade and the person you're with starts revealing more and more of his or her flaws (and vice versa). Writing is critical because you want to make sure you have a safe space where you can talk about any red flags, miscommunication, or incompatibilities you may notice. This will protect you from investing too much in a potential abuser or someone who doesn't share your values.

Meditating is a way you can take small breaks throughout the dating/entering new relationship process to connect back to yourself and who you truly are. Writing, reflecting and meditating also tends to give you an inner strength because you are challenged to use your own voice and interpretation rather than someone else's (which resists the gaslighting abusers might impose upon you). In addition, writing can help you also happily reflect on good times and when you go back to your journal over time, you'll be able to pinpoint moments of change, key conflicts, as well as communication or life skills you've been working on that have improved during the course of the relationship.

Schedule Me Time. Being in a new relationship can be taxing as much as it is energizing sometimes. Be sure to schedule at least a few hours to yourself every day where you unwind without being tethered to your phone and your new partner in crime. Take a long bath, read a good book, make a to-do list, watch your favorite show, listen to your favorite music, clean your room or dance in it — just do whatever you need to take a reprieve from that special someone and return to the truly special person that exists within you. It's essential to reconnect with that person every day, without relying on someone else to validate your existence constantly.

Hold off on physical intimacy until you're ready. There is a difference between physical intimacy and emotional intimacy. If you find that you often forget the difference and mistake the former for the latter, you're not ready for either. My recommendation for those who tend to rush into physical intimacy in past relationships and who have been in abusive relationships is to challenge yourself to wait a couple of months more than you usually do before you do anything that you would consider physically "serious" with someone. There is no rush to dive right into being physically intimate with someone especially if you've been in an abusive relationship in the past, because this type of intimacy will create a chemical bond whether you like it or not, making it more difficult to recover from a relationship that doesn't work out. This is not about viewing sex through a shameful lens; on the contrary, it's about protecting yourself emotionally and waiting until you are fully ready to engage in safe, fulfilling, consensual sex. By consensual sex, I mean that you're saying "yes" because you really want to say "yes," not because you're afraid to say "no." This goes back to challenging our people-pleasing behavior.

Casual sex is on the rise, and while that can be empowering for many women, it can also make women feel disempowered if they don't feel comfortable engaging in it. Don't follow social norms you're not comfortable with just to please the person you're with or go along with whatever society is saying. There shouldn't be a strict "timetable" that you need to follow as to when you're ready to have sex – it's whenever you feel ready. It doesn't matter what everyone else is doing. It's about what you want and deserve. Get to know the person first, because people will inevitably reveal their true selves in time.

You should never feel pressured to be physically intimate with someone until you feel emotionally ready to do so. In fact, if you do feel pressured or coerced, this may be a red flag that something is up. People who love, respect or care for you will not want to pressure you into something you're not ready for. If at a certain point you do become physically intimate, make sure that you always protect yourself. Do not ever give into the pressures to engage in unsafe sex or other dangerous physical activities. Remember that there are better partners out there who will not coerce you to do things or make you feel guilty if you don't do them. If your partner truly cares for you, he or she will make sure to listen to your concerns and communicate with you about what practices are best for both of you.

Check in with yourself about where this relationship is heading. Is it a positive, healthy relationship where both partners can communicate with one another without censure or belittling? Is it one that meets your needs? Are your values and lifestyles compatible? If there are major issues that are interfering with your relationship, make the time to address them right away. Don't leave it for later because things will build up and eventually explode in the end. If this is not the relationship you need and it's dragging you down, it's better to accept the pain now and end it sooner rather than later. Better to have had a three month relationship end than cling onto a three year relationship, where the investment and involvement is so much deeper and complex, thus more difficult to extricate yourself from.

Love yourself regardless of the outcome of any new relationship. Keep engaging in your self-care activities. Keep writing about your journey, on forums and on journals. Keep reading self-improvement books like these and the ones mentioned before. Keep pursuing your goals. Take deep breaths and repeat, "I love myself and I won't accept anything less than love, care and respect." Accept, respect and love yourself fully before expecting anyone to love, respect and accept you in a relationship. To be alone is a privilege and an opportunity to discover yourself and your greatness. Only when we've spent time alone can we know for sure that we've entered a relationship out of choice rather than loneliness or desperation. It is so key to remind yourself that life is too short to be abused or to be in an unhappy relationship. Life is too short to define yourself by others' opinions of you. Life is simply too short not to make your self-care a priority.

I know all of this advice is a lot to take in, so I've created a list of some important things to take away as you get to the ending of this book.

The Smart Girl's 10 Commandments of Self-Care and Self-Love

1. Remove the clutter from your life. This includes physical, emotional, and interpersonal clutter which only serves to detract you from focusing on your personal growth. Self-care and self-love require the space and energy to expand yourself, improve yourself and to reach higher levels of spiritual and psychological well-being. You can't achieve this by allowing unnecessary excess in your life. Clean the physical spaces where you live, because physical clutter can affect your mindset every day. An organized, tidy living space can do wonders for your mood and help you to complete tasks more quickly because everything has its place.

Cut the toxic interactions with people you don't need in your life which are only bringing you down. Stop allowing negative people to take up the space in your mind, heart and soul - they don't belong there and the ruminations you're engaging in over them are virtually useless. Refine your to-do list - stop trying to do a million things every day and instead, prioritize the main tasks which are most important to you and closest to what you value in life. Remember, quality beats quantity when it comes to self-care, so invest only in relationships and friendships that make you happier, pursue only the goals that are true to your deepest desires, and save your energy and talent for those worthy of you.

2. Give yourself unconditional love every day no matter what. Unfortunately, no one can really give this to you except yourself. Human beings, while capable of extraordinary love and compassion for others, still love others conditionally. When I say unconditional love, I truly mean unconditional, unlimited, infinite love. It may seem impossible to achieve, but do the best you can to love yourself regardless of whatever circumstances you may have in your career, relationships, status, power, finances, and so forth. As mentioned previously, I highly recommend reading the book *Love Yourself Like Your Life Depends On It* by Kamal Ravikant to understand how to enter into a mindset of self-love with a simple mantra.

Loving yourself unconditionally also means loving all of you - your flaws, your strengths, your secrets, your weaknesses. Every part of you is important, unique and worthy of love. When you give yourself unconditional love, you find yourself recognizing people who don't give you the full acceptance you deserve, which makes it easier to clean out the interpersonal clutter as mentioned above.

3. Take care, holistically. Creating a balance between work and play is essential to maintaining holistic self-care. Don't focus just on one aspect of your life when it comes to self- care. Energize your body, nourish your spirit, and enlighten your mind. Meditation is important for your spiritual, emotional and mental well-being. Yoga, pilates, dance cardio, and running are great ways to get into shape and improve your mood.

Eating mindfully will also help you to achieve optimal levels of energy and fitness while making your body less vulnerable to disease. Writing, reading and taking classes that interest you will keep your mind sharp, alert and always learning. Don't forget to maintain an active social life in the form of healthy relationships and friendships, as these are essential psychosocial resources that will serve as a crucial source of support and enhance your enjoyment of life.

4. Have high standards and stick to them. Self-respect is crucial to self-care because it protects you from settling for less when you deserve the best. This is toxic to how you view yourself and how you allow others to treat you, your values and your boundaries. If you allow others to trample over your expectations constantly, you're debasing your worth and chopping away at your self-esteem. You might be afraid that if you have high standards for yourself, people might perceive you as a high-maintenance person and even abandon you in the process.

Let them. It doesn't matter - in fact, it's probably a good thing that they do abandon you and reveal their true colors. At the end of the day, your opinion of yourself and what you deserve is all that truly matters in life. Having high standards in your career and relationships protect you in the long-run from scammers, emotional predators, and exploiters from sucking you dry and leaving you drained.

Think of things that fall below your standards as a bad business deal. You're not getting what you need and want out of it, but the person on the other side is. It's not worth the investment if someone else is benefiting from the positive return. Whatever your standards are, stick to them and don't let anyone or anything convince you to lower them.

5. Pursue your true passions. Life is too short to waste your energy and allocate resources into goals that are not truly your own. Caring for ourselves means remaining authentic and recognizing our true passions. Don't be pressured into picking a certain career path just because society says it's the right one for you; don't always settle for crappy jobs just because they'll pay the rent; don't pursue a major just because of its financial rewards unless it's something that really interests you. Sometimes you will have to make do with what you have in order to survive, but be sure you're still looking for ways to improve yourself and progress to something better and something that represents your true calling. For example, if you're a waiter who dreams of writing the next big screenplay, continue
working on it when you have the time. Setting aside time to pursue your dreams is important because these are things no one can take away from you. You own the right to all of your dreams and the ability to make them come to life.

The key is to still be practical, but also to be passionate. You were not meant to live this life doing just what is required to survive; you were meant to live life chasing your dreams. Don't be afraid of failure, because failure is a learning experience that will strengthen you and prepare you to do better in the future. Would you rather sit around and live in the regret of not knowing what would've happened if you had tried, or would you rather lead an exciting life by taking on risks and challenges that will ultimately lead you to what you were meant to do?

It's okay to explore multiple interests and talents; you don't have to limit yourself to one pursuit. However, if you do have that one dream that's been pulling at your heartstrings, start chasing it now. If you want to write a book, start by writing a blog or start writing the chapters to the book. If you want to go back to school, start looking up different programs. Take small steps today to start paving the path to tomorrow. Achieving long-term goals and big dreams are possible so long as you put the effort into making them happen. The most successful people I know are not just passive dreamers; they are active chasers who make an effort every day in order to accomplish their goals.

6. Minimize people-pleasing. Nobody wins when it comes to people-pleasing, except a person on the receiving end that's out to exploit you. Our tendency to people-please takes away from our authentic self, drains us of our energy, and deprives us of our ability to take care of ourselves in meaningful ways. By creating falsehoods in our relationships and interactions with others, we detract from who we were meant to be and pigeonhole ourselves into being who we're not just to please others. Be confident that who you are and what you want, feel, and experience are completely valid. You don't have to change to gain someone else's approval; if someone disapproves of you, that's okay. Like I mentioned in an earlier post, rejection is not about your self-worth - it's about another person's wants, needs and preferences. Don't see it as a selfish thing to honor your true self; it's not selfish, it's self-care and self-love.

7. Be mindful. Many of us go through life mindlessly and this detracts from our experience of present joy. This mindlessness is exacerbated by our fast-paced, technologically advanced society. We are so absorbed in social media and the buzz of our phone that we forget to appreciate the everyday, simple pleasures that come our way. The humming of the birds, the color of the sky, the beauty of someone's smile, the colorful and delicious food in front of us - these are all things we should be mindfully enjoying. Being attentive, aware and alert to our surroundings and the present moment is vital to experiencing each moment of life more fully and enhancing its joy. So make sure to take at least a couple of hours each day where you release yourself from the distractions of technology and enjoy nature, be engaged with whomever you're with, and immerse yourself in the conversation you're having. If you need help in doing this, start writing in a journal about the various things you observed during the day and how attentive you were to them. It takes practice to be more mindful in everyday life, but it's a worthy practice since it greatly enhances your experience of life's everyday moments.

8. Cultivate a lifelong habit of gratitude. Being grateful shouldn't be set aside for the holidays; it should be a way of life. Think of gratitude as another important component of mindfulness and as a lifelong habit that should be practiced every day. It teaches you to be mindful of the things you take for granted every day, from basic things like your ability to see and walk to the bigger accomplishments like having a good job, access to education or a supportive network of friends. Whether during times of strife or times of bliss, it's helpful to write in a gratitude journal and take note of all the things you have in your life – remember, these are the same things that other people may be praying for.

9. Give back to the world you live in. Remember how we talked about your unique talents and goals? This is one of the best incentives for exploring them. You are part of a larger world that needs your help. Whether it's through volunteering, research, activism, teaching, there are a myriad of ways to give. Find creative and engaging ways to help others whenever possible, whether its sharing resources or investing your time and energy into a cause you care about. You are here for a purpose and that purpose is tied to benefiting this world in positive ways. As you learn to love and care for yourself better, you'll also have more positive energy, love and compassion to give to those around you. Embrace your destiny and change the world.

10. Honor and validate your feelings. All of them. As someone who would qualify as a HSP (highly sensitive person) and an INFJ empath, I know how tough it can be to honor and validate your feelings in a world that's becoming highly desensitized to emotions and meaningful relationships. However, this last self-care commandment is perhaps the most important one of all. If you can't honor and validate your own emotions, you'll allow others to belittle and invalidate them, which means you're permit toxic people to enter your life without thinking twice. You'll make yourself vulnerable to gaslighting, manipulation, coercion and abuse. You'll settle for less because you believe that your feelings don't matter. Guess what? They do. You have to live with your emotions every day. That's why it is so vital that you learn to honor them.

Validate every emotion you have, even if you think it's inappropriate or "wrong" somehow. Emotions aren't meant to be rational, by the way. They are meant to be signals that provide information about situations you're experiencing or thoughts that you're having. Honoring and validating your emotions means telling yourself, "It's okay that I have these feelings. It's valid that I have them. These emotions are telling me something about this experience. Now I have a choice on how to react to them." You don't have to make your decisions based on your emotions alone, but you should consider them in the decision-making process when it comes to relationships, friendships and personal goals. Honor your feelings and you'll honor yourself. Congratulate yourself for taking crucial steps to better self-care and self- love!

HELPFUL TOOLS AND RESOURCES:

Tools and Information for Healing

http://www.huffingtonpost.com/author/shahida-arabi

&

http://everythingehr.com/healing-our-addiction-to-the-narcissist-an-interview-with-shahida-arabi/

The Gray Rock Method
http://180rule.com/the-gray-rock-method-of-dealing-with- psychopaths/

Signs of an abusive relationship
http://www.helpguide.org/mental/domestic_violence_abuse_type s_signs_causes_effects.htm#signs

Twelve core boundaries to live by in relationships by Natalie Lue
http://www.baggagereclaim.co.uk/12-core-boundaries-to-live-by- in-life-dating-relationships/

Self-Love Kit by Christine Arylo

http://madlyinlovewithme.com/self-love-kit/

Live Through This blog
http://livethroughthis.org/

Positive/Alternate Rebellion:
http://dbtselfhelp.com/html/alternate_rebellion.html

Alternatives to Self-Harm by the Sirius Project:
http://sirius-project.org/2011/08/16/distractions-and-alternatives- to-self-harm/

The Single Woman blog by Mandy Hale:
http://thesinglewoman.net/category/blog/

Twelve core boundaries to live by in relationships by Natalie Lue:
http://www.baggagereclaim.co.uk/12-core-boundaries-to-live-by- in-life-dating-relationships/

Self-Love Kit by Christine Arylo
http://madlyinlovewithme.com/self-love-kit/

Live Through This Blog
http://livethroughthis.org/

A Final Note

Always remember that the best revenge and the only revenge worth pursuing is self-love, self-care and success. Nothing and no one can defeat you if you choose never to give up. So, you must never give up on yourself, because you never know when a miracle might happen. Things can and will get better. Have hope; keep your boundaries firm, your values intact, but your heart open to the good that still exists in the world. I hope you've enjoyed taking this self- care journey with me. This journey is a lifelong one and I hope you continue to supplement it with many other books, forms of exercise, mindfulness and healing strategies that are available to you out there.

If you feel isolated or alienated, there are plenty of forums online as well as support groups that are waiting for you. If you feel hopeless, remember you are never alone and the best is yet to come. If you forget about the importance of self-care, re- open this book or the countless others I've recommended. If you feel voiceless like I once did, let the pen and paper be your weapons to victory. Start there and you will be astounded at how strong your voice truly is. I wish you all the best.

Take care,
Shahida

References

Alloy, L. B., La Belle, D., Boland, E., Goldstein, K., Jenkins, A., Shapero, B., Obraztsova, O. (2005). Mood disorders. In J. E. Maddux & B. A. Winstead (Eds.), *Psychopathology: Foundations for a contemporary understanding*. Mahwah, NJ: Lawrence Erlbaum Associates.

Arnett, J. J. (2000). Emerging adulthood: A theory of development from the late teens through the twenties. *American Psychologist, 55*(5), 469-480. doi: 10.1037//0003-066X.55.5.469

Brown, K. W., & Ryan, R. M. (2003). The benefits of being present: Mindfulness and its role in psychological well-being. *Journal of Personality and Social Psychology, 84*(4), 822-848. doi: 10.1037/0022-3514.84.4.822

Creswell, J. D., Way, B. M., Eisenberger, N. I., & Lieberman, M. D. (2007). Neural Correlates of Dispositional Mindfulness During Affect Labeling. *Psychosomatic Medicine, 69*(6), 560-565. doi: 10.1097/PSY.0b013e3180f6171f

Crowell, S. E., Beauchaine, T. P., & Linehan, M. M. (2009). A biosocial developmental model of borderline personality: Elaborating and extending linehan's theory. *Psychological Bulletin, 135*(3), 495-510. doi: 10.1037/a0015616

DBTSelfHelp: Life Skills For Emotional Health. Retrieved August 17, 2014, from http://www.dbtselfhelp.com/

Dooley, R. (2013, February 26). Why Faking a Smile Is a Good Thing. Retrieved August 19, 2014, from

http://www.forbes.com/sites/rogerdooley/201
3/02/26/fake-smile/

Ehlers, C. L., Frank, E., & Kupfer, D. J. (1988). Social
Zeitgebers and Biological Rhythms: A Unified
Approach to Understanding the Etiology of
Depression. *Archives of General Psychiatry, 45*(10),
948-952. doi:
10.1001/archpsyc.1988.01800340076012

Farb, N. A., Anderson, A. K., & Segal, Z. V. (2012). The
Mindful Brain and Emotion Regulation in Mood
Disorders. *Canadian Journal of Psychiatry, 57*(2), 70-
77. Retrieved August 17, 2014, from
http://www.ncbi.nlm.nih.gov/pmc/articles/PMC
3303604/

Gladding, R. (2013, May 22). Use Your Mind to Change
Your Brain. Retrieved from
http://www.psychologytoday.com/blog/use-
your-mind-change-your-brain/201305/is-your-
brain-meditation

Gotlib, I. H., & Joormann, J. (2010). Cognition and
Depression: Current Status and Future Directions.
Annual Review of Clinical Psychology, 6(1), 285-312.
doi: 10.1146/annurev.clinpsy.121208.131305

Haslam, M., Mountford, V., Meyer, C., & Waller, G.
(2008). Invalidating childhood environments in
anorexia and bulimia nervosa. *Eating Behaviors,
9*(3), 313-318. doi: 10.1016/j.eatbeh.2007.10.005

Malinowski, P. (2013). Neural mechanisms of attentional
control in mindfulness meditation. *Frontiers in
Neuroscience, 7.* doi: 10.3389/fnins.2013.00008

McKay, M., Wood, J. C., & Brantley, J. (2007). *The
dialectical behavior therapy skills workbook: Practical*

DBT exercises for learning mindfulness, interpersonal effectiveness, emotion regulation & distress tolerance. Oakland, CA: New Harbinger Publications.

Morrissey, P. J. (2013). Trauma finds expression through art therapy. Health Progress, 94(3), 44-47.

Pedersen, T. (2013, May 4). Meditation produces opposite effect of 'Fight or Flight' [Psych Central News]. Retrieved August 17, 2014, from http://psychcentral.com/news/2013/05/04/medi tation-produces-opposite-effect-of- fight-or-flight/54449.html

Rosenthal, R., & Jacobson, L. (1968). Pygmalion in the classroom: Teacher expectation and pupils' intellectual development. New York: Holt, Rinehart and Winston.

Seligman, M. E. (1972). Learned Helplessness. Annual Review of Medicine, 23(1), 407-412. doi: 10.1146/annurev.me.23.020172.002203

Spencer, S. J., Steele, C. M., & Quinn, D. M. (1999). Stereotype Threat and Women's Math Performance. Journal of Experimental Social Psychology, 35(1), 4-28. doi: 10.1006/jesp.1998.1373

Stout, M. (2005). The sociopath next door: The ruthless versus the rest of us. New York: Broadway Books.

Walker, P. (2013). Complex PTSD: From surviving to thriving: A guide and map for recovering from childhood trauma. Azure Coyote Publishing.

Van der Kolk, Bessel (2015). The body keeps the score: Brain, mind, and body in the healing of trauma. New York: Penguin Books.

Watkins, P. C., Woodward, K., Stone, T., & Kolts, R. L. (2003). Gratitude and Happiness: Development

Of A Measure Of Gratitude, And Relationships With Subjective Well-Being. *Social Behavior and Personality: An International Journal, 31*(5), 431-451. doi: 10.2224/sbp.2003.31.5.431

Winstead, B. A., & Sanchez, J. (2012). Cultural Dimensions of Psychopathology: The Social World's Impact on Mental Disorders. In J. E. Maddux & B. A. Winstead (Eds.), *Psychopathology: Foundations for a contemporary understanding* (pp. 45-68). New York, NY: Routledge.

ABOUT THE AUTHOR

Shahida Arabi is a summa cum laude graduate of Columbia University and the author of three #1 Amazon bestselling books, including *The Smart Girl's Guide to Self-Care, Becoming the Narcissist's Nightmare and Power: Surviving and Thriving After Narcissistic Abuse.* She studied English Literature and Psychology as an undergraduate student at NYU. Her interests include psychology, sociology, education and gender studies.

Her blog, Self-Care Haven, has been viewed almost 3 million times worldwide and her work has been endorsed by numerous clinical psychologists, mental health professionals and bestselling authors. She also blogs for The Huffington Post, Thought Catalog, and Psych Central. Her work has also been featured on The National Domestic Violence Hotline and DomesticShelters.org.

Visit her blog at selfcarehaven.wordpress.com, her website at selfcarehaven.org and join her Facebook community of nearly 50,000 self-care warriors at facebook.com/selfcarehaven.

58484890R00111

Made in the USA
San Bernardino, CA
28 November 2017